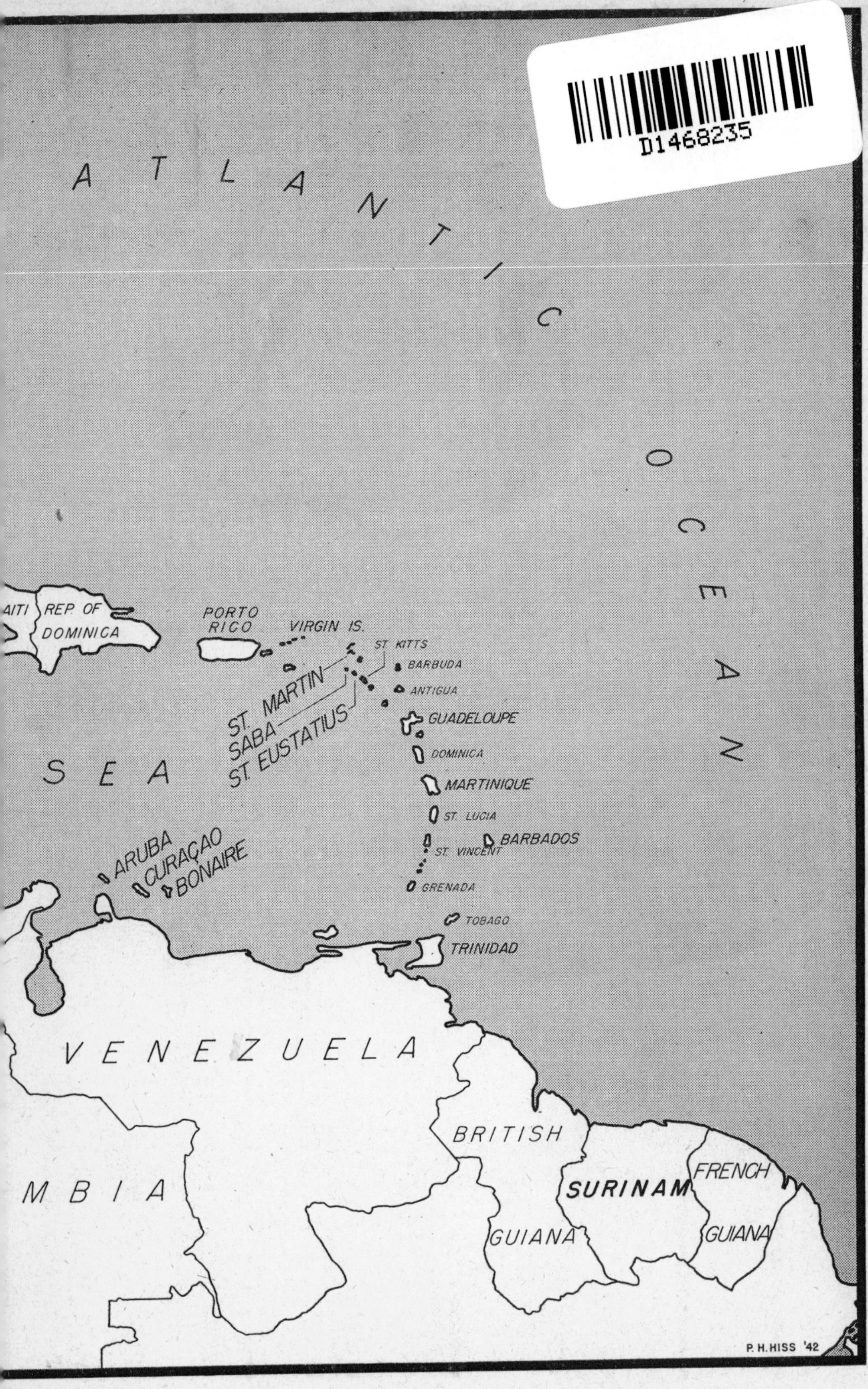

ATLANTIC OCEAN
AITI
REP. OF DOMINICA
PORTO RICO
VIRGIN IS.
ST. KITTS
BARBUDA
ANTIGUA
ST. MARTIN
SABA
ST. EUSTATIUS
GUADELOUPE
DOMINICA
MARTINIQUE
ST. LUCIA
BARBADOS
ST. VINCENT
GRENADA
TOBAGO
TRINIDAD
SEA
ARUBA
CURAÇAO
BONAIRE
VENEZUELA
MBIA
BRITISH GUIANA
SURINAM
FRENCH GUIANA
P. H. HISS '42

NETHERLANDS
AMERICA

Books by PHILIP HANSON HISS

BALI

NETHERLANDS AMERICA

NETHERLANDS
AMERICA

THE DUTCH TERRITORIES
IN THE WEST

PHILIP HANSON HISS

An Essential Book
Distributed by Duell, Sloan and Pearce, New York

To the Gallant Dutch People

Contents

vii

Illustrations

Illustrations

BETWEEN PAGES 114-115

BETWEEN PAGES 162-163

Appendixes

Preface

Curaçao and Surinam are familiar to those Americans who have traveled in the Caribbean, but the names of the small Dutch islands of Aruba, Bonaire, St. Martin, Saba, and St. Eustatius, which are not visited by cruise ships, will strike no responsive chord in the minds of most people.

In the past the Netherlands West Indies played an important part in American history. The first salute to the flag of the revolting American colonies was fired by the guns of Fort Oranje at St. Eustatius, and Oranjestad, the capital of the island, was the transshipment port for more than half of the arms and ammunition sent from France to America, and which sustained the American revolutionists in their struggle for freedom.

The Dutch and the American people have always had in common a passion for freedom, and it is probably this that prompted the Dutch to become our allies during the Revolution. This is not the only debt of the United States to the Netherlands. We have only to look around us to be reminded of Dutch contributions to American culture, which are out of all proportion to the small number of Dutch immigrants to this country. There is ample evidence of their influence in our art and architecture.

Today Holland is under the heel of the Nazis and the Japanese have overrun the Netherlands East Indies. The Dutch Territories in the Western Hemisphere alone fly the Dutch flag. Small though they are, they are playing a vital part in the cause of the United Nations. The refineries of Curaçao and Aruba supply a large percentage of the high-octane gasoline used by the Royal Air Force, and the bauxite mines of Surinam are the source of much of the aluminum ore so important to the war industries of the United States.

The Territory of Curaçao, with an area of only 364 square miles and a population of slightly less than 120,000, is composed of the islands of Curaçao, Aruba, Bonaire, Saba, St. Eustatius, and the southern part of St. Martin. The first three are called the Leeward or A B C Islands; the others, which lie five hundred miles to the northeast, the Windward Islands, a fact that has caused some confusion, as they fall within the British Leeward group.

It is likewise confusing that the same name should be applied to both the Island and the Territory of Curaçao, and a change is contemplated after the war in the Dutch nomenclature. The Territory will probably be designated Gebiedsdeel Curaçao and the Island Staatsdeel Curaçao.

The name of St. Martin, which was formerly called Sint Martijn by the Dutch, was changed in 1936 to Sint Maarten, but I have retained the French-English spelling, which is far more familiar to most people.

Surinam, on the northeastern coast of South America, with an area of 55,527 square miles, was more important than Curaçao prior to the American Revolution, and it was well known to the captains of sailing ships from New England. In spite of the fact that it is far larger than the total area of the islands comprising the Territory of Curaçao, its population is only fifty per cent greater. Most of its area is covered by uninhabited virgin jungle.

Curaçao and Surinam together form the most interesting colonial possessions in America.

This book is the direct result of five months spent in the Netherlands West Indies from December 1941 to May 1942, when, through facilities accorded to me by the Netherlands Government, I was able to study the economy of these Territories and their preparations for defense. I was also able to travel far into the interior of Surinam. Many previous trips to the East and the West Indies provided a background against which the fruits of the present trip could be evaluated.

Since my return, research has proved unexpectedly difficult. Much information has not been available, and, in other cases, it has been hard to separate legend from fact. For this reason, the publication of *Netherlands America* has been unavoidably delayed.

I would like to express my thanks to the many officials of the Netherlands Government whose hospitality I have shared and who have helped me in so many ways. My particular gratitude is due to His Excellency, Prof. Mr. J. C. Kielstra, Governor of Surinam; to His Excellency, Mr. G. J. J. Wouters and His Excellency, Dr. Piet Kasteel, the past and present Governors of the Territory of Curaçao; and to Dr. N. A. C. Slotemaker de Bruine, Director of the Netherlands Information Bureau in New York, and the staff of the Information Bureau.

I am also indebted to Dr. D. A. IJsselstijn, General Manager of the Royal Dutch Air Lines, and to Mr. H. E. Kies, Director of the Royal Netherlands Steamship Company, for greatly simplifying my transportation problems.

I am deeply grateful to Mr. Jan van Essen for his companionship on many trips around the island of Curaçao; to Mr. G. H. Polvliet, who unselfishly put at my disposal his knowledge of Curaçao; to Prof. Gerold Stahel, Director of the Government Agricultural Experiment Station in Paramaribo, who made all of the arrangements for my trip up the Surinam River; to Father Vitus Brenneker, whose enthusiasm for the Indian pictographs on Bonaire and for the people of the island was so contagious; and to Mr. A. van Meerten, Director of the Government Schools in St.

Martin, who contributed to my knowledge of the folklore of the Windward Islands. In closing, I give my sincere thanks to my good friend Frank R. Crumble, Jr., who shared with me both the difficulties and the enjoyments of the greater part of this trip.

PHILIP HANSON HISS

New Canaan, Connecticut
   September 21, 1943

The Setting

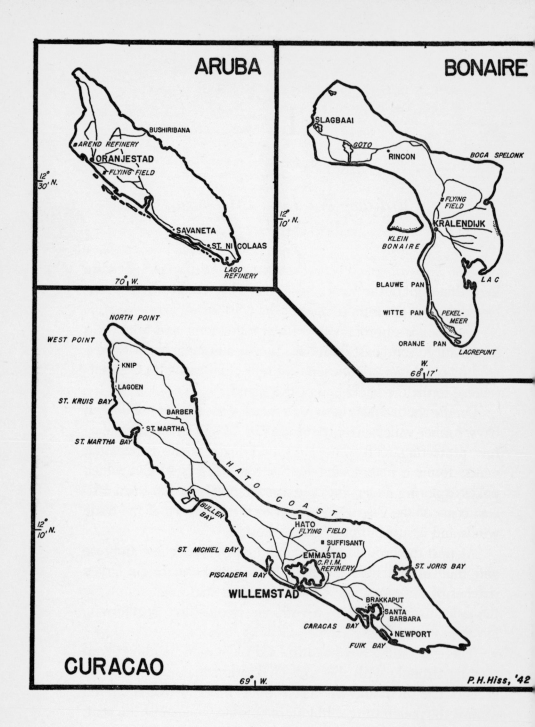

ARUBA

BUSHIRIBANA

AREND REFINERY
ORANJESTAD
FLYING FIELD

12° 30' N.

SAVANETA
ST. NICOLAAS

70° W.

LAGO REFINERY

BONAIRE

SLAGBAAI
GOTO
RINCON
BOCA SPELONK

12° 10' N.

FLYING FIELD
KRALENDIJK

KLEIN BONAIRE

LAC

BLAUWE PAN

WITTE PAN
PEKEL-MEER

ORANJE PAN
LACREPUNT

W. 68° 17'

NORTH POINT

WEST POINT

KNIP
LAGOEN
ST. KRUIS BAY
BARBER
ST. MARTHA
ST. MARTHA BAY

HATO COAST

12° 10' N.

BULLEN BAY

HATO FLYING FIELD
SUFFISANT
ST. MICHIEL BAY
EMMASTAD
C.P.I.M. REFINERY
ST. JORIS BAY

PISCADERA BAY

WILLEMSTAD

BRAKKAPUT
SANTA BARBARA
CARACAS BAY
NEWPORT
FUIK BAY

CURACAO

69° W.

P.H. Hiss, '42

1

Curaçao—The Leeward Islands

CURAÇAO, Aruba, and Bonaire lie within sight of the Venezuela coast. They are brown and sunbaked against the intense blue of the Caribbean Sea.

Curaçao is approximately forty miles long and runs in a northwest to southeast direction. Its volcanic base is partly covered by coral reefs, and a series of hills culminating in Christoffelberg forms the backbone of the island.

On the south coast there is a remarkable series of landlocked bays, former valleys, where the sea has broken through the narrow protecting reefs. The largest of these is the Schottegat, which forms a magnificent harbor for Willemstad and which pokes exploring fingers into the surrounding hills, but the northeast coast of the island is exposed to the full force of the trade winds and is surf-buffeted and harborless.

Against the brown of the island the brilliant yellow and rose and blue of the little Curaçao houses and the bright green patches of the occasional Chinese gardens stand out, supplying the color usually associated with the tropics that is otherwise lacking.

There are still a few beautiful old plantation buildings, contrasting strongly with the new civilization that has grown up around the oil refineries. Their thick outer walls, shuttered against the penetrating sunlight, are protection against the heat,

3

and inside the large central rooms, the atmosphere is one of cool twilight even on the hottest day. The out-buildings, former slave quarters and corrals, usually are grouped close to the houses. Such plantations as Santa Barbara and Santa Marta are landmarks, and the former, claimed by many to be the oldest house on the island, is said to have been built for the Spanish governor before the Dutch occupation.

The native houses are even more typical of Curaçao than the plantations. Most of them are simple rectangles, with thick clay walls and roofs of either thatch or tin. There are variations in the materials used, but little if any in the shape. Some of the poorer people living in the vicinity of the C. P. I. M. refinery have built their houses of flattened gasoline tins, but even these houses are freshly painted in brilliant colors and are scrupulously clean inside and out. A house may form a single room or be divided into two, or even three rooms.

The typical Curaçao house is surrounded by a cactus hedge, and there is usually an excuse for a garden—a small patch of sorghum and beans—and the inevitable livestock—goats, pigs, and chickens. But the average Curaçao garden is as drab as the surrounding landscape, and it is only the hard-working Chinese who have been able to turn the prevailing color from beige to green.

The Chinese garden patches form a startling contrast by the very brilliance of their color. The dusty earth has been turned to a rich brown by constant watering, and rows of tender shoots spring up between the furrows. A pool of water is in the center of each garden and at all hours of the day and night the untiring Chinese can be seen dipping water into cans slung from poles carried across their shoulders and running down the furrows sprinkling row after row. Their remarkable results lead one to believe that with irrigation much might be accomplished on the island.

Elsewhere the soil is baked hard by the sun, so that the infrequent rains run off quickly and often do much damage. Shallow dams have been built across the ends of gullies and depressions to catch the water and allow it to sink into the ground instead of flowing into the sea, and long lines of windmills—not the picturesque Dutch type, but modern galvanized iron ones—are features of the Curaçao landscape.

Life in Curaçao centers about the harbor at Willemstad, where half the island's population lives. The city is divided by St. Anna Bay, a narrow channel which forms a highway for ships through the heart of the city into the Schottegat. Entering St. Anna Bay on a large ship is very much like riding up Fifth Avenue on the upper deck of a bus. One looks directly into the windows of the office buildings and down onto streets crowded with pedestrians and automobiles.

The harbor of Willemstad is unusual, but the pontoon bridge which joins the two sections of the city, Poenda to the east and Otrabanda to the west, is unique. The life blood of the island is oil from the Maracaibo basin of Venezuela, and the coming and going of the tankers controls the life of Willemstad, for the bridge may remain open for an hour at a time. When this happens, long lines of automobiles form in front of the Hotel Americano and the Government House.

Pedestrians can cross St. Anna Bay by launch when the bridge is open, but automobiles must either wait or make the long trip around the Schottegat. There is talk at the present time of building a bridge across the bay or a tunnel under it, but the estimated cost of three million dollars would scarcely be repaid.

The original pontoon bridge was designed by a former American consul to Curaçao, and at one time, when it was owned by a private company, a toll of two cents was charged to persons wearing shoes, one cent to those wearing sandals, while those without shoes were allowed to cross free. Tourists amused themselves by crossing barefooted, an innocent pastime, but one that has been spoiled by the Government, which has since built a new bridge which it operates without charge.

St. Anna Bay is all-important. Sloops and schooners from Venezuela and Colombia, Panama and Trinidad, Santo Domingo and Haiti cluster about its docks. Beyond lie freighters, corvettes, and tankers, and where the bay widens into the Schottegat it discloses the huge, sprawling C. P. I. M. refinery, with its ever-present plume of blue smoke flying like a banner to the southwest.

Willemstad was established shortly after the Dutch took over the island of Curaçao from the Spaniards in 1634. The original site of the city was the present district of Poenda, to the east of St. Anna Bay, but as the city grew, it spread across the bay to a new section, which was called Otrabanda, or Overzidje: literally—"other side." The Waaigat, an arm of St. Anna Bay extending to the east, limited Poenda to a narrow peninsula, but the growth of the city has forced it across the Waaigat into a new residential district named Schaarlo. Pietermaai is a further development to the east of Poenda.

The narrow streets of Poenda were originally wider, but the houses were crowded together for protection in the days of international rivalry and privateering. Balconies at first were built over the streets, but supports later were extended to the ground and the areas walled in, adding to the houses but turning the streets into narrow chasms.

Poenda is dark and mysterious at night. The occasional sound of a guitar mingles with the raucous blasts from a dozen radios, musty smells emanate from the houses, and dust blows about in little eddies. Here an oil lamp discloses an old shoemaker still at work, and there a corner bar is filled with seamen. Chinamen in undershirts and loose trousers slip from one doorway to another, while an open window reveals a Negro dance in progress, gaiety and sound filling the room.

People bring chairs into the streets and sit outside of their houses smoking and talking, and one catches occasional glimpses through open windows of rooms with rows of rocking chairs against the walls and artificial flowers decorating the tables. Paintings and mottoes, often in English, speak of the religious nature of the people.

In the darkness the ships moving in and out of the harbor seem huge and amorphous and along the quayside sloops and schooners rock gently at their moorings, oil lamps hanging from the booms casting faint shadows that spring into life with the recurring swells. But in the sunlight the houses of Willemstad are a kaleidoscope under a cobalt sky accented by fleecy cumulus. The prevailing colors are saffron and pink and blue for it is against the law to paint any house white, due to the intensity of the light.

Buildings two centuries old, with stepped gables and balconies, vie with offices and theaters of modern design. But much of the beauty of Willemstad lies in its old buildings, the Government House, the Protestant Church, the old Jewish Synagogue, and the Water Fort, to name a few, and a great deal of its charm will have been lost when modernism has robbed the city of its individuality.

The population of the Caribbean islands long has been cosmopolitan, but the island of Curaçao has been even more of a melting pot than the others. This is due first to the extraordinarily liberal policy of the Dutch, who from the beginning allowed both freedom of religion and freedom of enterprise, and second to the many races that have come to work in the oil refineries.

The original population of Curaçao was Indian, and the island has been in Spanish, British, and Dutch hands. Many slaves were brought from Africa, Portuguese Jews came from Brazil, and as a great port it has attracted Syrians and Chinese and men from Madeira and the Azores. More recently there have been Negro immigrants from the other Caribbean islands. Forty-five races in all are said to be represented.

Papiamento, the native language of Curaçao, reflects the cosmopolitan composition of the population. It contains Indian, African, Spanish, Portuguese, Dutch, English, and French words, but the Spanish influence is strongest, due to the island's proximity to Venezuela.

Curaçao is truly liberal in its feelings about race and color. Everyone has equal rights and equal opportunities. Everyone born in Curaçao is considered a Curaçaoan, except those whose parents are employed in the oil industry. Oil-company employees remain outsiders, partly because of their attitude to the islanders, partly because their salaries are out of all proportion to the earnings of the rest of the population, and partly because the people working for the oil companies never really make Curaçao their home.

There is no discrimination against race or color in Curaçao, but there is a definite resentment to any reference to color by an outsider. This is an oversensitivity, a realization that discrimination exists in the outside world, and an ever-present fear that it will find its way into the life of the island.

Aruba is physically different from Curaçao only in degree. It is the smallest of the A B C islands, the driest, the flattest, and it has the least vegetation. But unlike Curaçao, Aruba has been Americanized, for hundreds of Americans have come to live in St. Nicolaas and to work in the huge Lago refinery.

Until twenty years ago Aruba was a mere dependency of Curaçao, an island with a rural population engaged in small agriculture, cattle raising, and the panning of gold, whereas today the island has something of the cosmopolitan atmosphere of Curaçao, but it has neither Curaçao's color nor its background.

Oranjestad, the capital of the island, is a mixture of the old and the new. It has wide, paved streets, modern government offices, and excellent stores. But Fort Zoutman is a relic of the past, and the quayside and careenage are filled with sailing vessels from Curaçao, Venezuela, and Panama.

St. Nicolaas could not be more different. Whereas Oranjestad is typically Dutch, St. Nicolaas could be described as frontier-American. The town is a hodgepodge of dirt streets, wooden shacks, Chinese restaurants, saloons, and a few shops that would not be out of place in Paris or London. It sprawls in disorderly fashion up to the very gates of the refinery, which forms a dramatic background, with its tall stacks, spheroid tanks, piers, and machine shops, and extends to the west along the coast road toward the Savaneta military camp, which can be seen in the distance.

The census of 1816 showed that there were still 564 pure-blooded Indians on Aruba. But today of the original population neither pure Indian nor pure Negro stock exists. There has been a fusion of the two racial strains, and it would be impossible to say which has absorbed the other, for the Indian influence is here stronger than in the other Dutch islands.

During the last hundred years the Indian language has died out and has been replaced by Papiamento, which differs from the Papiamento of Curaçao in that it contains a higher percentage of Indian and American words.

In spite of Aruba's atmosphere of desolation, the western shore of the island has a South Seas look. It is bordered by coconut palms which fringe beaches of fine white sand—the only really good beaches on the Dutch islands—and the southwestern coast is protected by a coral reef which has been blasted in two places to form the entrances to the harbors of Oranjestad and St. Nicolaas.

The northwestern district of the island, which is best suited to agriculture, contains a large percentage of the rural population. A road runs inland through low hills covered with cactus and huge boulders, and the red earth blends with the soft green-gray skeletons of dried bushes.

At Bushiribana the ruins of a gold smelter stand starkly in the midst of a desert swept clean by the salt-laden air, and at Balashi are more ruins: the ghost of a gold mine, rusted remnants of machinery, the skeletons of buildings, and empty tanks.

At Boca Prins gleaming white sand dunes contrast dramatically with black, overhanging cliffs and a tumult of dark blue water churned to white and palest green, where the long swells —built up by the trade winds across five hundred miles of open sea—buck the black honeycombed face of the cliff and fall back shattered or sweep sibilantly across the white sand and recede, leaving an impermanent border of lacy foam.

It is only forty-two miles by sea from Willemstad to Kralendijk, the capital of Bonaire, yet the distance, measured in terms of material civilization, is enormous. Curaçao is modern in the same sense that a city in the United States is modern. There is always a sense of urgency and bustle. The streets are crowded with automobiles, the quays lined with ships, the shops filled with wares from Europe and Asia and America. But Bonaire is rustic and simple and altogether charming. Dirt roads, winding through cactus hedges, pass small, neat houses painted brilliant yellow or the even more typical red, and their fanciful names

Paradise, Thank God, Immaculate Virgin, Saint Peter, God Will Reward Us, or *Jerusalem,* clearly indicate the overwhelmingly Catholic nature of the population.

Bonaire's salt ponds are still worked in the same primitive way as when the island was used as a penal colony for free Negroes and mulattoes who were set to work gathering salt as a punishment. There has been little change on the island during the three hundred years of Dutch occupation. Today a steamer periodically ties up to the pier at Kralendijk, and there is an infrequent plane service; but most traffic is still carried on by schooner and sloop, and far more people travel on foot than in automobiles. Bonaire has been able to retain its rustic atmosphere in spite of the rapid growth of its sister-islands, Curaçao and Aruba, only because it is less accessible and because it has no really good harbors.

The population of Bonaire, unlike that of Curaçao and Aruba, is largely rural, and many of the people do not go farther from their farms than is necessary to draw water, except on Sundays, when they may walk for two hours to go to church. As in Aruba, Indian blood is clearly noticeable in the faces of the people.

Bonaire is shaped like a boomerang, its ends pointing west and south, and cradled within the center of the bow lies Kralendijk, with the small, low, uninhabited island of Little Bonaire just offshore.

The countryside is literally covered with cactus. Cactus fences line the roads and separate the fields, and in the uncultivated areas are cactus forests. The most important cash crop of the island is aloes, a plant which resembles cactus, grows well in the dry sandy soil, and requires very little attention. The goats, which run almost wild on the island, will not touch it, for it is bitter and has medicinal qualities.

Bonaire is drier than Curaçao, and water is brought from

wells to the houses on people's heads or on the backs of donkeys.

The northern section of Bonaire is mountainous and sweeps abruptly down to the Rincon plain, from where a series of low foothills continue in a general east-west direction and end close to Kralendijk. A conical hill rises out of a green plain near Onima, its slopes covered with huge slabs of limestone, and here again one sees the terracing that is so noticeable along the northern coast of Curaçao.

The southern arm of the island rises only a few feet above the level of the sea and from the air it appears to be almost awash. The coast road south of Kralendijk soon becomes a mere track skirting salt marshes along the shore. Salt crystals gleam on the sand and the track often divides and climbs the sides of dunes. There are no houses, and the countryside is a desolation of low shrubs stunted by the salt air; and it is so flat that the sand dunes by the sea appear to be miniature hills.

South of Kralendijk is the Blauwe Pan, where a blue obelisk by the waterside once served as a guide for ships coming to Bonaire to load salt. Farther along the coast there are white and orange obelisks. Beyond the Blauwe Pan scenery becomes more interesting. The gleaming sand imperceptibly merges into water tinged with cerise and lavender marking the salt pans of Pekelmeer, a shallow lake that stretches for miles along the southwest coast of the island with only a narrow beach separating it from the sea. The light shimmers on the face of the water, and the heat rises in visible waves, destroying reality and imparting to the scene a dreamlike quality. The orange and white obelisks, the windmills of the salt factories, and the lighthouse at Lacrepunt at the southern tip of the island, dissolve and reappear as if suspended in the air, and the low shrubbery bordering Pekelmeer becomes a forest by the distortion of light and then floats divorced from both earth and sky.

At Witte Pan huge piles of crystalized salt wait to be ground in the mill. Nearby are the small stone huts, mere kennels in which a man can just stand up or lie down, and which were once used to house the slaves who worked in the salt pans. A few of these tiny houses have been newly roofed and are in use today. Though one must bend double to go inside them, and though there are no windows, they are not really uncomfortable. They are grouped close to the white obelisk and adjoin an abrupt beach of white coral that resembles bleached bones and upon which the sea dashes in short, angry bursts, while overhead pelicans patrol tirelessly, and occasionally plummet into the water.

Even more interesting than the pelicans are the flamingoes which wade in the Pekelmeer and make their nests on its northern shore. Their brilliant, beautiful red feathers at first are seen only as a deeper reflection of the lake's surface; but any sudden noise startles them, and after a few quick strides, they rise in flocks of fifty or sixty with long necks and legs extended and circle to settle again only a short distance away.

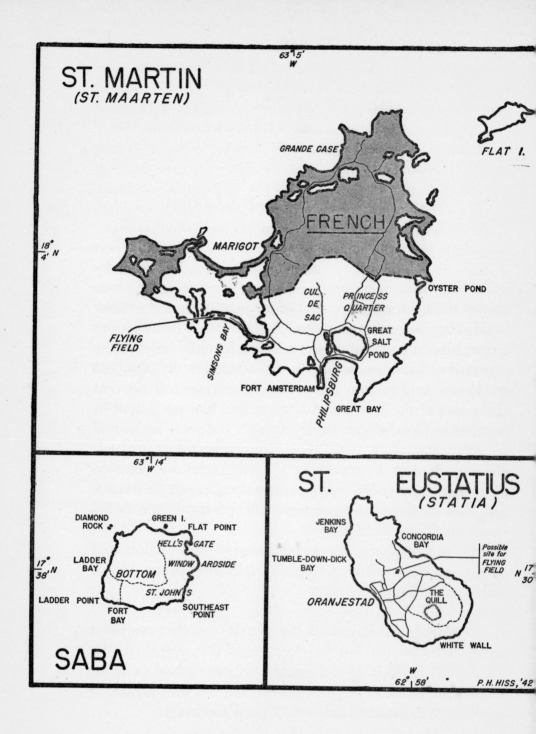

ST. MARTIN
(ST. MAARTEN)

63° 5' W

GRANDE CASE

FLAT I.

FRENCH

18° 4' N

MARIGOT

OYSTER POND

CUL DE SAC

PRINCESS QUARTER

GREAT SALT POND

FLYING FIELD

SIMSONS BAY

FORT AMSTERDAM

PHILIPSBURG

GREAT BAY

SABA

63° 14' W

DIAMOND ROCK

GREEN I.

FLAT POINT

HELL'S GATE

LADDER BAY

BOTTOM

WINDWARDSIDE

17° 38' N

LADDER POINT

ST. JOHN'S

FORT BAY

SOUTHEAST POINT

ST. EUSTATIUS
(STATIA)

JENKINS BAY

CONCORDIA BAY

TUMBLE-DOWN-DICK BAY

Possible site for FLYING FIELD

ORANJESTAD

THE QUILL

17° 30' N

WHITE WALL

W 62° 58'

P. H. HISS, '42

2

Curaçao—The Windward Islands

T<small>HE</small> Netherlands Windward Islands—St. Martin, Saba, and St. Eustatius—form so strong a contrast to the Leeward group that they might be part of another world. They lie midway between St. Thomas, in the American Virgin Islands, and British Antigua, five hundred miles to the northeast of Curaçao, and are mere dots among the islands of the Lesser Antilles, forming only seven and one-half per cent of the area of the Territory of Curaçao and four per cent of its population. These islands lie off the main steamship routes and are today almost forgotten. Communication between the islands and with the outside world is by sloop and schooner; however, an airport is under construction at Simsons Bay on St. Martin, and, after the first of the year, there will be a regular service between St. Martin and Curaçao.

The people of the Windward Islands speak English, and have taken their culture from the neighboring British islands and from the United States.

St. Martin, the largest of the islands, is only twenty-one square miles in area, but despite its small size, it is shared by France and Holland. It is the only Caribbean island to be divided between two European powers, and it is the only one of the three Windward Islands with a good anchorage.

15

The extended arms of Great Bay enclose the roadstead, and mountains spring up steeply from either side of Philipsburg, which lies on a narrow sand bar between the Bay and the Great Salt Pond. The deep blue of the sea is shot with sunlight and dark patches of color, and shadows from passing clouds dull the gleaming white of the beach.

The sand bar on which Philipsburg is built is no more than a hundred yards wide and a mile long, and it rises only a few feet above the sea. In the more than two hundred years since it was founded the town has been damaged by several hurricanes and in 1819 it was almost destroyed. But it was rebuilt, and today there are about two hundred houses fronting on the two streets which run the length of the bar. The main street is wide and paved with cement. It has narrow sidewalks on either side, and the buildings, which abut one another, are mostly two-storied and many have balconies. This gives the effect of a narrow chasm ending in a mountain wall at either end.

St. Martin epitomizes the condition of the Netherlands Windward Islands, which live with their memories of the past in a state of suspended animation. Many of its plantations are deserted, and the more virile elements of its population have emigrated. The people who have remained exist largely on money remitted to them by relatives in Curaçao, Aruba, and the United States. Many people are supported by government projects, and though they are not lazy, they have become apathetic.

The soil is not particularly fertile; much of it is tipped at an angle of forty-five degrees and many of the fields are covered with huge boulders. Sugar and cotton, cultivated during the days of slavery, have been abandoned, and only a small amount of hay is baled and shipped to Curaçao. Even the salt industry, which once made the island important, has all but vanished, due to competition from the neighboring British island of Anguilla.

St. Martin is a pleasant, peaceful spot. Its population is

kindly and hospitable, but like so many Caribbean islands, it has been unable to discover its proper niche in the economy of the twentieth century.

Saba, the smallest of the three Windward Islands, has less than half the area of the island of Manhattan. Its volcanic slopes plunge abruptly into the sea. It is the greenest of the Dutch islands, the quaintest, and the most dramatic.

Nowhere at the base of Saba's towering cliffs is there space for a village or a garden plot; but as the early settlers must have foreseen, this was a protection, and the history of the island records the repulse of several attacks by no other means than stones hurled down upon the raiders.

Fort Bay Landing, on the south side of the island, is the official anchorage. It is a few hundred square yards of relatively level ground composed of the detritus washed down an old lava flow on the mountainside.

There is no pier at Fort Bay or at Ladder Bay, on the western side of the island, and it still is necessary to land on the beach in a small boat rowed by skilled oarsmen. The difficulties and dangers of landing have been overemphasized by sensational writers, but split-second timing is the alternative to a good wetting.

There are no wheeled vehicles on Saba, due to the precipitous nature of the island, and until recently everything, including building materials and even pianos, was "headed" up the mountain. The importation of donkeys a few years ago caused a strike among the porters, who felt that their livelihood was threatened. Now, in the words of S. J. Kruythoff in *The Netherlands Windward Islands,* "The donkeys carry many of the loads. The owners draw the pay and spend a lot of time and energy packing grass on their heads to feed the donkeys."

It takes less than half an hour on foot or on horseback to reach the town of Bottom, which nestles in the green cup of an

extinct volcano. Its neat houses are surrounded by brilliantly
colored shrubs and flowers. The crater wall sweeps upward to
the heights that are named for St. Crispin, the patron saint of
shoemakers, for in the beginning of the eighteenth century there
were so many shoemakers on the island that it was even suggested that its name be changed to St. Crispin. At that time
there were more cattle on Saba than there are today, and shoe-
making has died out, due to the lack of hides, the declining
population of Saba and the surrounding islands, and the increase
in the mail-order business.

The crater wall is a deep green, with here a garden patch
and there a banana grove. Higher, the vegetation becomes more
dense and is lost in the clouds which race over the summit of
Mt. Scenery.

Saba, alone among all the islands of the Caribbean, has a
population that is predominantly white. Its people are the descendants of the same families which settled the island three
hundred years ago. Due to the limitations placed upon agriculture by its precipitous slopes, the number of slaves on Saba
never exceeded the white population.

There has been no recent white immigration and consequently no new infusion of blood for many years. Emigration,
however, has taken place almost wholly among the white population, who have found it necessary to seek work outside of the
island. During the nineteenth century and the early twentieth
century many white Sabans found employment in the United
States Merchant Marine and became well known for their sea-
manship, but because of recent restrictions on immigration and
labor in the United States, opportunities of this kind have
dwindled. For much the same reason, seasonal employment on
the sugar estates of the Greater Antilles has disappeared, and

Curaçao Belle.

St. Anna Bay, Willemstad.

Conga Dance at the Curaçao Sports Club.

Refinery Worker.

Industrial Phantasy.

Miles of Pipes—C.P.I.M. Refinery.

Tall Towers.

More Than A Million Gallons Storage.

Phosphate Plant, Newport.

Windward Coast of Curacao

Harbor Entrance, Willemstad.

Pietermaaistraat, Willemstad.

British Trench Mortar Squad in Action.

First U.S. Troops in Curaçao.

Santa Barbara Plantation.

Native Hut.

Beautiful Old Curaçao House.

Coast Defense Gun, Willemstad.

Native Transportation.

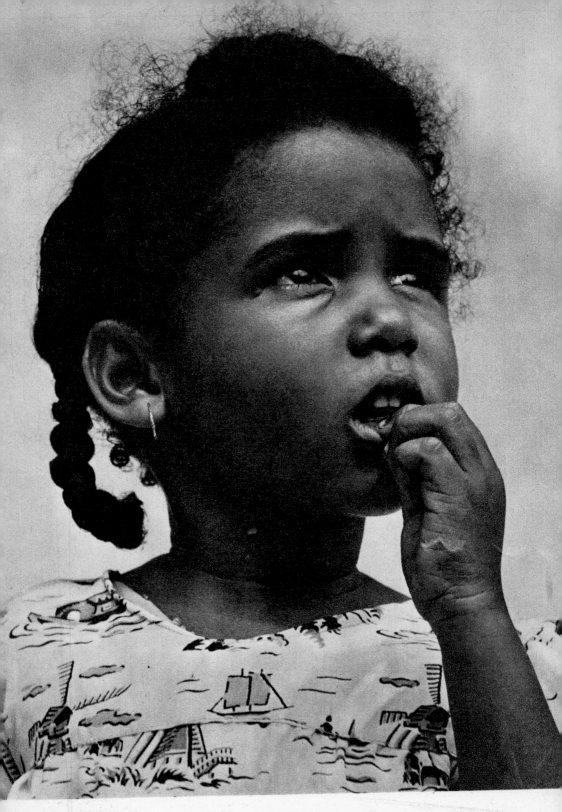

Negro Child.

the refineries of Curaçao and Aruba are now the chief sources of outside employment.

Few Negroes have left the island, and as they are more prolific than the white population, they have consequently gained in numbers and in percentage until today the population stands almost equally divided between blacks and whites. But there has been little miscegenation.

The white population of Saba is still robust after many generations in the tropics. The only marked example of deterioration was in the small village of Marypoint, which was isolated on the western side of the island and was accessible only by a very bad trail. Marypoint consisted of seven families, all with the name of Sagors, and, as was to be expected, generations of inbreeding and an inadequate diet had had their effect. Several years ago the Government moved the entire village to Bottom, where their houses were reassembled in a district called "The Promised Land," and the children are now able to attend school regularly.

Another colony of white settlers at Simson's Bay on the island of St. Martin has had a similar history. These people, who are largely fishermen, remained almost isolated until 1933, when a bridge was built connecting Simson's Bay with the mainland. This colony showed the same symptoms of inbreeding noticed at Marypoint, and most of the people suffered from hookworm. Signs throughout the village today proclaim that it is "prohibited to walk barefooted in Simson's Bay," and the people have been given medicine. The health of the colony recently has shown great improvement.

Strenuous physical labor in the fields and carrying heavy burdens on the steep trails have kept the white men of Saba in good physical condition, but the women, who exercise little, have not fared so well. Mr. Krugers, the Administrator of the island, attributes the degeneration of the women to their diet, which consists mainly of potatoes, bananas, cassava, fish, biscuits or bread, and tea, supplemented by a few beets, carrots, cabbages, onions, and peas. He claims that, owing to the importation of mail-order catalogues, the interest of many of the women is now directed toward the latest fashions, instead of to the food they eat, and that too much money is spent on clothes at the expense of health. The income of many Saba women also has been reduced in recent years because needlework once sold in the United States recently has been virtually excluded by high tariffs.

White supremacy in Saba over so many years has been possible only because the island is tempered by almost continual breezes from the sea, and because the settlements are situated at an altitude of from 800 to 1,600 feet above sea level. Windwardside, with an almost entirely white population, is at 1,400 feet and is often quite cold at night. The absence of malaria and other tropical diseases has been an equally important factor. The physical characteristics of the Negroes, however, make them naturally better adapted for work in the tropics, and with their inevitable acceptance of a lower standard of living, it is a foregone conclusion that they will one day inherit the island.

Bottom is the seat of government, and at one time the white inhabitants considered themselves the elite of the island, but today it has a large percentage of Negroes. Bottom lies within the crater, but Windwardside, Hell's Gate, and St. John are on the eastern slope of the island, where they look down hundreds of feet onto the cloud-flecked, ever-changing surface of the sea. To the north the mountains of St. Martin break the even circle of the horizon and the serrated peaks of St. Barts barely rise above the water. To the east, scarcely fourteen miles away, lies St. Eustatius, and beyond, St. Kitts and Nevis.

The men of Saba are excellent sailors, through years of experience in launching their small boats against the heavy seas and in beaching them under all conditions. They are also boat builders of some ability, but the myth that Sabans build sloops—or even schooners—on the tops of mountains and lower them over the cliffs is ridiculous. A few boats are still built, but they are so small that they can be carried on the shoulders of a dozen men.

Many Sabans are fishermen, and their stout little boats can be seen on the mere shelves which serve as beaches. "Shelves" is an apt word, for not only do the mountains drop steeply to the sea, but they fall away with equal abruptness under water, so that there are few good anchorages, and even the largest ships can approach within a few feet of the shore.

The legend of Saba as an island of beautiful, golden-haired women with blue eyes is in a class with the story about shipbuilding on the mountain tops. It simply is not true. These stories doubtless originated with travelers who were astonished to find white women living in the Caribbean, and while it is true that the women are white and that many are attractive, some writers have so far improved the story as to state that ninety per cent of the population are women, and that there is only one eligible bachelor on the island. Recently a young United States Navy flier on patrol duty, intrigued by this tale, dropped a letter addressed to "the most beautiful girl in Saba." His success was immediate, and weeks later he was still receiving answers from the various competitors for the title. As a matter of fact, the women outnumber the men on Saba by only a small percentage.

Agriculture on Saba is a precarious means of living, for the mountain slopes are strewn with boulders which are a source of danger to the houses because of constant erosion of the soil. When they become insecure, it is necessary to brace them or to drop them into holes. It even seems as though the gardens must break loose and slide into the abyss below.

Under these circumstances it is strange that people earning good salaries elsewhere should choose to return to the unremunerative work of extracting a living from Saba's soil. But Sabans have a very strong attachment to their island and almost all look forward to returning some day. It is a unique and beautiful spot.

St. Eustatius is the most desolate of the Windward Islands, and even its dramatic past is slowly being obliterated by the wind and the sea. Fort Oranje, which fired the first salute to the rebel flag of the American colonies, still looks down on the bay that was once crowded with blockade runners; but the warehouses, which played such an important part in American history, now lie in ruins, their disordered stones mingling with the spume and the fine black sand along the beach, in a losing battle against the encroaching sea.

Fort Oranje houses the Government offices and the wireless station. Adjoining it lie the roofless ruins of the Dutch Reformed Church, its tower rising dramatically among the graves, and close by is the yellow-brick ruin of the Jewish synagogue. There are a few other buildings of stone or brick, mellowed with age and surrounded by trees, but most of the houses are of wood.

The streets of Oranjestad have recently been paved, but beyond the town there are only a few dirt roads winding through the brown stubble and the sparse undergrowth.

The Quill rises in an almost perfect cone to form a background for the town. It is an extinct volcano, and an author of one hundred and fifty years ago has described its upper slopes as being desolate and the rest of the southeastern part of the island as being entirely under cultivation. But the sugar and the sisal plantations have been deserted and the upper slopes of the Quill are the only suggestion of green on the island. Everywhere else there is only dust and ruins and silence—a silence broken at long intervals by the faint sound of the surf. The dust rises in little clouds and its gray mantle falls on the undergrowth which hides a wall or the ruins of a building.

A few rusting cannon recall the days when it was indeed "The Golden Rock," but St. Eustatius has outlived its past, and a feeling of decay is uppermost. What ghosts must haunt these mountains! What thoughts of buried treasure must trouble the dreams of the people! What is the power that holds them to this rock, which has turned from gold to the dull, gray color of dust?

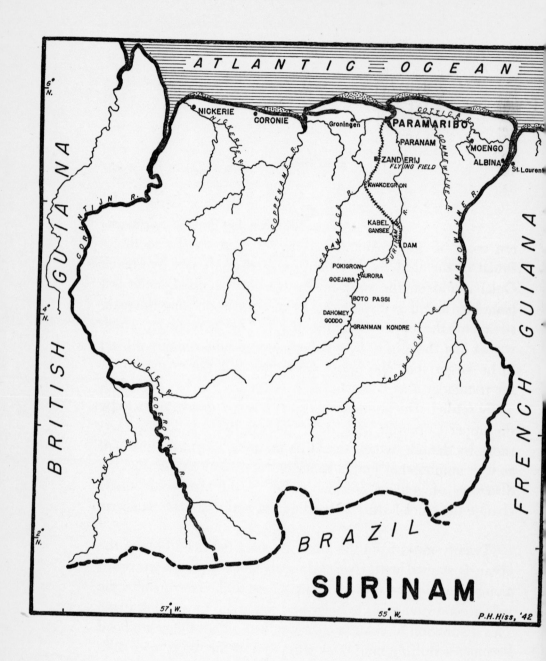

3

Surinam

Surinam lies on the northeast-
ern coast of South America. It is bounded on the south by
Brazil, on the north by the Atlantic Ocean, on the east by French
Guiana, and on the west by British Guiana, though the last
boundary is still in dispute due to an error in defining the main
stream of the upper Corantijn River. The New River, which
was at first thought to be a tributary, was subsequently proved
to be larger than the upper Corantijn, and the ownership of
the triangular area between the two rivers never has been defi-
nitely settled. The boundary, however, is commonly taken to be
the upper Corantijn, and the Dutch are likely to lose the territory by default, which would be no great loss at the moment
as it is uninhabited jungle in an inaccessible location, but the
discovery of gold or precious stones in the area could easily
change the official attitude from one of carelessness to concern.

Twenty miles from the Surinam coast the deep blue of the
ocean is stained with river sediment which is swept westward
along its mangrove-studded shore. Close to the river mouths the
pale green water turns to beige and is marked by a line of foam.
This distinction of color is clear-cut, but where the ochre flood
becomes a shifting mud bank rising out of the sea is more difficult to judge. Nor is there any certain demarcation between

25

land and water, for at high tide the sea creeps into the uninhabited swampy area along the coast.

From an approaching ship the coast of Surinam looks no different today than it did in the year 1500, when members of Columbus's third expedition landed on its shores. The broad yellow river-roads disappear into the jungle, winding through the deep green of tropical rain forests broken only by occasional Bush Negro and Indian villages. The outlines of abandoned plantations are softened by secondary growth and in places are almost entirely obliterated, but even in the days of greatest prosperity, cultivation did not extend more than a mile from the rivers, except in the vicinity of Paramaribo.

Here and there the green roof of the jungle is obliterated by low clouds, and rain beats with staccato fury onto the tangled mass of foliage and leaves a million tiny craters in the yellow water.

The narrow coastal plain is crisscrossed by rivers and canals which are the only means of communication throughout most of the country, and many of the coastal rivers are so deep that they can be navigated for some distance by steamers.

The general direction of the rivers in the interior of Surinam is from south to north, but close to the coast the majority flow in a westerly direction, because the ocean currents sweeping west from the Amazon have deposited silt at their mouths and have added considerably to the original land area. It is possible to traverse this network of rivers from the French to the British borders by way of Wane Creek, the Coermatibo, Cottica, Commewijne, and Surinam rivers, the Saramacca Canal—the only man-made link, Wanica Creek, the Saramacca, Coppename, and Wayombo rivers, Arrawarra Creek, and finally, the Nickerie River.

A few miles from the coast there is a narrow zone of savannas, and beyond—the unrelieved jungle stretching to the Brazilian

border. Much of this jungle is uninhabited or is thinly populated by nomadic Indians or by the Bush Negroes.

Seven-eighths of the population of Surinam lives in the narrow coastal belt into which all of the agriculture and industry of
the colony is crowded, and of these one-third lives in Paramaribo, the capital.

Paramaribo is situated on a shell reef on the west bank of the
Surinam River about fourteen miles above its mouth. It is a
sprawling town that is recognizably Dutch in character, for it is
intersected by canals, and the countryside close at hand is diked.
Everywhere that the Dutch have gone they have waged un-
ceasing war against the sea.

Many of Paramaribo's streets are lined with mahogany,
flamboyant, and tamarind trees and royal palms, and during the
day the multi-storied, wooden houses are shuttered against the
heat. These houses form a strong contrast to the colorful architecture of Curaçao, but what they lack in color is more than
compensated for by the exotic crowd in the streets.

The jungle has cut off the Guianas from the rest of South
America, and there has been no Spanish or Portuguese influence.
Instead, Negroes and Madeirans, Javanese and British Indians
have come to the country, and the streets of Paramaribo are
crowded with a heterogeneous throng of Negro women in gay
Kotta Missie costumes, bearded and turbaned British Indians,
Hindu women wearing saris and with jewelry set into their
noses, and tiny, inconspicuous Javanese.

The focus of official life is the Gouvernementsplein. To the
northeast of this square is the governor's residence, and to the
northwest, framed by tall trees, a few lovely, mellow brick
buildings reminiscent of the Dutch colonial architecture of New
England: the Hof van Justitie, the Administratie van Financien,
and the Gouvernement's Secretarie. To the southeast, just be-

yond the Gouvernementsplein, lies Fort Zeelandia, which once stood guard over the city. All of these buildings are clearly recognizable in prints of Paramaribo dating back to the eighteenth century.

To the southeast of the square is the Palace Hotel, and a short block beyond is the river, which makes a great arc from south to east so that the entire waterfront is clearly visible from the eastern end. The K.N.S.M. and Government piers lie in the center of this arc, and Saramaccastraat, where Bush Negroes from the interior come to trade timber and wood carvings for gunpowder, tobacco, and cloth, is farther to the west.

The streets of Paramaribo are dusty and there is a moldy smell about the houses. At night they are dimly lighted and quiet.

Native troops drill in the Gouvernementsplein early in the morning; Dutch farmers drive by in their high, two-wheeled carts, bringing their milk into the city for delivery, the hoofs of the horses beating out a staccato rhythm on the hard ground; and water trucks sprinkle the streets, their spray raising little clouds of dust that are quickly beaten down. Sometimes a Dutch woman passes on a bicycle, a child strapped to the small seat behind her, and, always at the same hour, the Government officials walk to their offices, their white suits freshly starched and gleaming in the sunlight; at two o'clock they return, their day's work done.

Of the smaller towns, Nieuw Amsterdam is so close to Paramaribo that it has been overshadowed. It is the administrative center of the Commewijne District, and reached its greatest importance during the slave rebellions. Fort Amsterdam, the most interesting landmark, was built in the eighteenth century after Cassard had pillaged the colony. Though it was of great importance in earlier times it is now deserted.

Nieuw Nickerie, the second city of Surinam, is the center of an important rice-growing district largely populated by Javanese and British Indians. The town originally was built in 1820 on a shell reef at a point between the Nickerie River and the sea and was called Nieuw Rotterdam, but the currents along the Surinam coast are forever changing the contour of the land, and this village was washed away by the sea. It was rebuilt in 1870, but the second village also was destroyed by the sea, and in 1879 the town of Nieuw Nickerie was built about five kilometers from the mouth of the river. There is no shell reef at the present location, and the site of the town had to be endiked and drained.

Nieuw Nickerie has a population of slightly more than 4,000, and it is growing in importance, though it is cut off from communication with the other districts except by ship or river launch.

Coronie has been even more isolated than Nieuw Nickerie for it was surrounded by immense swamps and could be approached only from the sea, but a road to Paramaribo now is being built. Construction was started at both ends of the road at the same time and has reached as far as the Coppename River on the Coronie side and to Carel François on the Saramacca River from Paramaribo. The remaining fifteen kilometers between Carel François and the Coppename River are now under construction, but it is estimated that it will take two years to complete this short distance. Much of this road runs through swamps, and like the majority of Surinam's roads, it has been raised above the surrounding land by first constructing a base of heavy clay, which is allowed to dry out, and on which the road proper, consisting of sand dug from shell reefs, is laid down. This forms a compact surface that is passable in all but the worst weather.

When the road is completed, much of the charm that arises in Coronie's isolation will be lost, but the town still retains its

Old World atmosphere. Many more women wear the Kotta
Missie costume so typical of Surinam, with its long full skirt and
its bustle and wide starched collar, which it is claimed was originated by the Moravian missionaries. It is typical of the Mother
Hubbard introduced by missionaries into so many other countries, but the Surinam Negress has given it a flair all her own.
She fashions it out of cloths of brilliant colors and bold designs
and tops it off with a matching headkerchief, which is tied in
many ways to indicate the mood of the wearer.

Coronie's single long avenue is lined with coconut palms and
its many old graves testify to the fact that it was colonized by
the Scotch during the eighteenth century. The plantations still
go by the names of Inverness, Hamilton, Perseverance, Tote-
ness, Friendship, Burnside, Hope, and Walton Hall, though the
original families have either died or have gone away. Many of
the plantations, which originally grew cotton, are deserted,
others have been given over to coconuts, and recently the
swampy area has been planted with rice by British Indians and
Javanese.

Many people in Paramaribo speak of Coronie's charm. They
describe the beautiful palm avenue and the old Scottish graves,
and some recite in detail the difficulty of coming ashore in
a small boat and then having to cross the mud flats on a "mud-
horse," a flat board with a box seat, which is propelled from behind by a Negro kneeling on one leg and pushing with the
other. But very few people have actually been to Coronie. It is
just too much effort to travel in Surinam, and many people who
have lived in Paramaribo for years have never been more than
twenty kilometers out of the city.

Albina is a dreary little frontier town, eighteen miles above
the mouth of the Marowijne River, which forms the boundary

between Surinam and French Guiana. Opposite to Albina and separated from it by only a mile of water is St. Laurent, one of the largest of the French penal colonies.

Albina was once the chief city of the Marowijne District, but the district commissioner has moved to Moengo, which has become important because of its bauxite mine. It is thirty-one miles to Albina from Moengo but the road is a mere track through the jungle and the savanna. Rutted, narrow, and deep in mud, it climbs short, steep ridges and plunges through chasms cut through the green wall of trees, so that two hours is the minimum time required for the trip.

Albina remains as a garrison post and as the point of departure to the gold fields on the Lawa River, a week's trip by Bush Negro *corial,* or dugout. What little color the town possesses is due to the colony of transient Bush Negroes who carry freight to the gold fields and to the existence of several Amerindian settlements in the vicinity.

The main street of Albina parallels the river. There are the military barracks, a row of two-storied wooden houses, the Government offices, a few general stores run by Chinese and natives, and a number of residences. Close to the pier there is a little park, and beyond a number of Bush Negro *corials* drawn up on the river bank, but there is nothing to mark Albina as different from a hundred outposts buried in the South American jungle. It is not particularly Dutch in character, and there are many Brazilian towns similar in every detail.

The yellow walls of the prison at St. Laurent are clearly visible across the mile-wide Marowijne River. They are an unpleasant symbol of oppression, and every year men who have not sunk so deep in misery that they have ceased to care, make their escape into Dutch territory. The authorities do not send them back so long as they are law-abiding and willing to work. But although there are few Dutchmen who are sympathetic with the French conception of penology, many of the prisoners have become incorrigible and, in the interests of Surinam, must be returned.

Albina remains in my mind as a symbol of the essential difference between Dutch and French rule in Guiana. On one side of the Marowijne River there is freedom; on the other, subjection, inhumanity, and the death of hope.

Most of Surinam's 55,000 square miles are covered by dense jungle in which only the Amerindians and Bush Negroes live. The Amerindian population numbers only 2,026, according to Government figures, and each year it diminishes, but the Bush Negroes are increasing, and are estimated at 19,032. These Bush Negroes are the descendants of escaped slaves, and they are divided into five tribes, which have received their names from incidents in the slave insurrections of one hundred and fifty or more years ago.

The Saramaccaners form by far the largest tribe, numbering twice as many as the others together. They inhabit the Surinam River from Kabel Station to the confluence of the Gran Rio and the Pikien Rio, and there are several Saramaccaner villages on each of these tributaries. A number of Saramaccaners also live on the lower Saramacca River close to Paramaribo.

The Aucaners—inhabiting the upper Commewijne River and the Marowijne and Tapanahoni rivers—are the only other tribe of importance. But there are also three smaller tribes, numbering only a few hundred each—the Matawaais on the upper Saramacca River, the Quintee Matawaais on the middle Coppename River and its tributary the Tibiti River, and the Paramaccaners, living on the west shore and on some of the islands of the middle Marowijne River.

In addition to the Surinam Bush Negroes there are also the

Bonis, who fled across the French border during the slave insurrections and have remained in French Guiana ever since.
They live on the east bank of the Lawa River.

The cultural influences of all of these tribes having been
similar in their native Africa as well as during the period of their
enslavement, their language, art, and religion differ only slightly
today, and the most interesting thing about them to an anthropologist is that their present civilization is almost identical with
that of Africa in the seventeenth century.

To enter the jungle is to be transported into another world.
Here the rivers are the highways, and only narrow trails overarched by tall trees lead to the villages and to the provision
grounds. The river banks are a mass of tangled lianas and dense
undergrowth. Here and there a huge silk-cotton tree raises its
head above the level of the jungle. These trees are sacred to the
Bush Negroes and an especially fine one frequently marks the
entrance to a village.

Bush Negro villages are often at the heads of rapids, a vestige of the days of slavery, when the churning water formed a
natural fortification, and many villages and provision grounds
still are hidden from the river, another survival from the slave
insurrections.

Life among the Bush Negroes is uncomplicated. At the head
of each tribe is a *granman*—literally, great man—appointed by
the Governor of Surinam, and under him are the captains of
the various villages, each of whom is assisted by several *bassias*,
or bosses. The role of the *granman* and the captains, however,
is only nominal, and the real power is wielded by the heads of
family groups. Conduct is determined by traditional law, which
is largely African in origin. Bush Negro society is matriarchal,

a fact that the Bush Negroes characteristically justify with the remark that, "After all, who can tell who the father of a child really is?"

Bush Negro villages have streets of hard-packed earth bordered by groups of palm-thatched huts, their roofs sloping almost to the ground. The walls are of woven palm fronds and many of the low entrance doorways are elaborately carved, but the huts have no windows.

Each group of huts belongs to a *mbe,* or matriarchal family group, and a man having more than one wife must provide a hut for each wife and her children. If he can afford it, he has a treasure house or *godo woso,* where he keeps his personal belongings free from the prying eyes of his wife or wives. He may have a storehouse for produce, and some families have shrines for the family gods. In most villages there are also a few community buildings, a council house, and shrines for the various deities and for the ancestors.

The huts frequently are divided into two rooms, the front room being used as the living quarters and the back for sleeping. Sometimes a fire for cooking is built in one corner of the front room, although there is no vent in the roof for the smoke to escape, and on rainy days the entire roof of a house appears to be steaming. At other times the cooking is done in a communal cooking shed.

The doorways of the houses are no more than four feet high and are pivoted so that they squeak loudly when they are opened. An enemy entering in the night can be heard and as he has to bend over he can be easily dispatched.

Clothing in the jungle is simple. Young children of both sexes go naked and older ones wear only a small piece of cloth held in place by a cord. Men ordinarily wear a loincloth, and for dress occasions, a *camissa*, a toga-like garment often made of many colorful bits of cloth joined together like a patchwork quilt, which is worn over one shoulder and carried under the opposite arm. The women dress in a cloth, or *pangi*, wrapped around their torsos and reaching from the waist to the knee, and in the cool of the evening another cloth is thrown over their shoulders. Both men and women wear amulets, bracelets, and necklaces, as well as arm and leg bands woven from cotton. A few women wear brass wire or rings around their legs which they keep shiny by polishing them with sand.

Cicatrization is a common form of decoration, though it is found more often in the remote villages than in those close to missions or to civilization. The scars are made by slashing the face and body in set designs and by rubbing charred rice hulls into the open cuts, which leaves black marks against the brown skins. They are called *cutti-cutti*, or *kamemba*, and are supposed to have erotic significance.

The Saramaccaners and the Aucaners both let their hair grow long and braid it into fanciful designs.

The Bush Negroes exist by hunting, fishing, and by agriculture. They hunt with bows and arrows and whenever possible with shotguns and rifles, and they fish with bows and arrows, with lines, and with a poison, *nicou*, which stupefies the fish and allows them to be caught easily. A few Bush Negroes have also learned the use of fish traps from the Indians.

Agriculture in the jungle is difficult. Provision grounds must be hacked out and the fields burned over. The soil of the jungle is not particularly fertile, and the heavy rains leach out the mineral salts, further reducing its productiveness.

The Bush Negroes cultivate yams, bitter cassava, peanuts, maize, dry rice, and a little sugar cane, but their method of cutting new provision grounds next to the old ones has led to great difficulties with umbrella or leaf-cutting ants, which attack the newly planted fields.

Umbrella ants do not exist in the virgin jungle, and the Amerindian method of agriculture, whereby a new provision ground is cut in a new location well removed from the old one, is much better than the Bush Negro method, and the Amerindian grounds do not become as heavily infested with ants in a period of four or five years as the Bush Negro fields in a single season.

When a new village is started the provision grounds are made close to it, but as each year a new ground is cut behind the old one, the provision grounds of many villages are ten to fifteen kilometers distant, and it is not possible to cultivate them and return to the village in the same day; consequently temporary huts must be built next to the grounds.

The reckless agricultural methods of the Bush Negroes have made life increasingly difficult for them because they must continually rove farther from the rivers in search of unspoiled land.

The Bush Negroes are an interesting and colorful people, but their importance has been grossly exaggerated. It is not strange that they have been able to adjust themselves to life in the jungle, for the jungle is mysterious only to the white man. It is an almost exact counterpart of their native Africa, and, as many slaves escaped after only a few years of bondage, they brought with them an undimmed knowledge of jungle lore.

The Bush Negroes have retained their African culture because they have been isolated, but basically they differ very little from the town Negroes of Paramaribo or the Negroes of the West Indian islands.

They speak a language called the *Saramacca tongo,* sometimes referred to as *deepi-tahki,* whereas the town Negroes

speak *tahki-tahki,* or Negro English, and natives of Curaçao
speak Papiamento. All of these languages have an African construction, but whereas the *Saramacca tongo* is composed of
words with a strong Portuguese influence, *tahki-tahki* is to an
English-speaking person almost understandable, and Papiamento reflects the more cosmopolitan influences of Curaçao,
with its Spanish, English, and French terms.

The Bush Negroes have retained the art of wood carving
from their African heritage, but the merits of their carving have
been greatly exaggerated and carved objects are not nearly as
much in evidence as one is led to expect. Much of this work
now is done for sale in Paramaribo.

The Bush Negroes appear at their best as boatmen on the
rivers, where they are removed from civilization and its influences, but at heart they are no longer magnificent savages ex-
hibiting contempt for the white man and his ways. They are
in fact only too anxious to enjoy the comforts of civilization and
to exchange their bows and arrows for guns and their hand-
woven cloth for imported cottons.

Music and dancing are the threads that bind the Negro to
his past, and the Bush Negroes, town Negroes, and island
Negroes are all fully responsive to its intoxication.

Dancing to drums is forbidden by the authorities in Curaçao, but it nevertheless continues in the more remote districts.
An ordinary social dance is called a *dansi-dansi,* but dancing to
drum music is called *bongo* or *tamboer* dancing. Of two dances
at Mahoema one was held inside a cabin and the other outdoors.
At both dances a man poured out a small glass of white rum
for each person, who tossed it off with a single gulp. The drum-
mer sat on a bench and people formed around him in a semicircle clapping their hands and chanting. The only instrument
other than the drum was a *wiri-wiri,* the iron head of a hoe,

which is held in one hand and struck or rasped with a metal
rod held in the other hand. Several times women danced within
the semicircle, the backs of their wrists placed against their hips,
their elbows turned out, and sometimes children danced together, their hips moving suggestively; outside of one cabin a
tiny child, not more than two years old, imitated her sister.

The dances of the town Negroes of Paramaribo and of the
Bush Negroes differ surprisingly little from those of Curaçao.

In Coronie I watched two dances called *seketi* and *soesa*,
and on the upper Surinam River I saw the same dances and
others as well, but even the famed *winti* and *kromanti* dances
show little variation from the limited African repertoire of steps,
and they are interesting because of their frenzied tempo and because they often lead to trance rather than for their choreg-
raphy.

In the Surinam jungle, where it has remained unchecked, belief still exists in various African deities, though voodoo takes a
slightly different form than it does in the Caribbean.

Superstition is manifested among the Bush Negroes in various ways: by the use of amulets; by the *azang*, or magical spirit
barrier of palm fronds placed before the entrance to every village which brushes away the evil spirits from a visitor entering
the village; and by beliefs such as the one forbidding anyone to
mention the name of a rapids until it has been passed, lest the
god of the river become angry. Witch doctors still practice their
rites and retain their power over the imaginations of the people,
and there are magic villages, such as Dahomey on the Surinam
River, that may not be visited by white men.

African superstition in Curaçao has been modified by the influence of the Catholic Church and by the unemotional attitude
of the Dutch.

In Bonaire in the years when there has been more rain than

usual and there has been a good harvest, a harvest festival with masquerading and music called *Simadan* or *Simadam* is celebrated during the New Year's holidays. This has very strong Catholic connotations coming as it does on a Christian holiday, and it is similar to harvest festivals in Europe. The same festival is called *Seu* in Curaçao, but it is only in Bonaire that masquerading takes place.

These ceremonies are reminiscent of *Ra-ra-di* in Haiti which combines Christian and African concepts.

One needs only to spend a few days with the natives of the Dutch islands to realize that the more extreme manifestations of African superstition are absent, and that there are no orgiastic ceremonies. Yet, the belief in the power of charms remains. Many ideas are imported from the surrounding Caribbean islands, and in Curaçao there is a belief in zombies, or ghosts, and there is a certain amount of hocus-pocus such as the placing of egg shells, hair, small mirrors, or shells close to the house of an enemy. But in Curaçao one seldom hears of death by black magic, and the conclusion is that these charms are used for lesser ends.

In Saba both Negroes and whites believe in witchcraft, and it is not unusual for the gezaghebber, or administrator, to receive a report that men in white have been seen walking about the mountain and knocking at the doors of houses. This is especially true after a death, when all houses are kept tightly closed.

A great deal of money is spent in the Windward Islands on obeah men and on visits to the neighboring French and British islands for charms to cure the sick or to discomfit an enemy.

The people of the Windward Islands have many odd superstitions, and during my stay on St. Martin, Mr. A. van Meerten, Director of the Government Schools, recounted them to me. A number of them are worth repeating:

To keep away jumbees and zombies, the following means are effective: Place a horseshoe on the front door; burn rubber or human hair in the room; sprinkle a mixture of salt and urine on the doorstep; put some blood of a butchered ram on your head; or bury the head of a sheep, goat, or other animal under a lime tree, which is considered to be a dwelling place of good spirits. The last remedy insures perfect peace at night. As an extra precaution, however, every door and window must be closed tightly at night. Write the names Melchior, Balthazar, and Gaspar on the windows. This combined with sprinkling salt and urine on the doorstep is the most effective.

If some people touch you with a special piece of wood you "go absolutely stupid." An eyewitness recounted that a boy who had been so touched was told to act as a donkey. He obeyed, walked on all fours, and even brayed. Later he did not remember anything that he had done.

Certain passages from the Scriptures may be used to cast a spell, but it is necessary that the victim be told that a spell is being put upon him. Other passages will break the spell.

"Black-heart" books from New York are used to "cast bad luck" on others.

A spirit cannot follow you if you walk downstairs backwards. In houses having only one floor, the spirits live over the ceiling.

All kinds of herbs, burned hair, even menstrual blood, are mixed with soup as a love potion. "After that he will follow you wherever you go, even over a hill."

The devil can be evoked by dances, but one word from the Bible will stop him.

Thefts may be detected by going to an obeah man, who looks at the photograph of a suspected person and goes into a trance. These obeah men usually come from Guadeloupe or Nevis. They can make a person crow like a cock, or make other animal noises

—for a dollar. They sell charms for any purpose and are equally willing to sell a counter-charm to the victim.

An amusing incident recently occurred in St. Eustatius. A Negro accused of theft had to appear before the judge, but he had put a charm in his shoe and was confident of cheating justice. Unfortunately for him there were a number of mosquitoes in the room, and the judge took up a flit gun and sprayed the room close to the prisoner, who was convinced that this was a counter-charm and immediately confessed.

The Period of Development

4

Discovery and Settlement in the Caribbean Area: 1492-1650

Cᴏʟᴜᴍʙᴜs's ships arrived off Watling Island in the Bahamas on October 11, 1492. On the following day his sailors landed, and the primitive peace of these islands was shattered forever. A few days later Columbus sighted a large island to the south, and because it reminded him of the coast of Spain, he named it Española.

There has been considerable discussion as to the purpose of Columbus's first voyage, some people maintaining that his intention was merely to search for islands in the Atlantic Ocean—perhaps the fabled Antilia which appeared on maps of the fifteenth century, others insisting that he was seeking a shorter passage to India. But whatever the original object of his voyage, it is certain that he believed the newly discovered islands to be part of India, for he called the inhabitants Indians, and, as it was several years before his assertion was disproved, the name persisted. Later they were called the Antilles by the Spaniards.

At the time of their discovery the Antilles were inhabited by three Indian tribes, each with a distinct culture: the Ciboney, living in Western Cuba and Haiti; the Arawaks or Tainos, who had at one time inhabited the entire area from Brazil to Florida, including the West Indian islands; and the Caribs, a warlike tribe originating in the interior of Brazil, who were the traditional enemies of the Arawaks, and who occupied the Lesser Antilles and made sporadic raids into the larger islands, where they killed the men and carried off their women. The word "Carib" is a corruption of "Cariba," which means a valiant man, and our word "cannibal" is derived from "Caribal," the name used by Columbus.

The Arawaks were not a single tribe, but a group of related tribes of similar linguistic stock. They were agriculturists, and the name "Arawak" is said to mean "meal eaters," because cassava was their staple food. We find evidence of their civilization today in stone axes and pictographs.

The Ciboney, on the other hand, lived chiefly on sea food, though they raised a little cassava, and it is they who left the shell heaps found in the West Indies.

None of these tribes possessed a high degree of civilization. They had no architecture, little art, and the most primitive forms of music. Most of them lived in caves and wore only loincloths.

The Indians of Española welcomed Columbus and his sailors. These Indians were kindly, simple people with no ambitions, but they soon paid dearly for their naiveté. Great numbers were captured and sold into slavery, and others were forced to labor in the mines which the Spaniards quickly opened, and from which they expected to amass great wealth.

The Indians were not accustomed to the exhausting physical labor exacted by the Spaniards, and many died as a result. Others committed suicide, and many rose in arms against their oppressors, but they were quickly hunted down and killed.

In 1519 an epidemic of measles and smallpox, against which the native population had no resistance, destroyed more than half the remaining population of many villages. Within a quarter of a century of the Spanish occupation of the islands, the Indian population was reduced from an estimated 300,000 to a few thousands.

The Spaniards were quick to realize the importance of their discoveries in the Western Hemisphere and to protect them. Pressure was brought on the Pope, and in 1493 the first of several Papal Bulls was issued, recognizing Spain's exclusive right to all lands discovered in the Western Hemisphere.

In the following year, on June 7, by the Treaty of Tordesillas, Spain and Portugal divided most of North America, South America, and Africa between them. That the other European nations did not recognize Spain's right to these possessions made very little difference, for Spain was at that time the most powerful nation in Europe, and her fleets sailed the seas at will.

There has been a great deal written about the cruelty and avariciousness of the Conquistadores, and very little mentioned about their ability to colonize. While it is perfectly true that Spain's primary object was plunder, subsequent exploitation would have been impossible had not the foundations of her early settlements been well laid. The first Spaniards brought with them many European plants. Among these was sugar cane, which was to affect so greatly the later history of the Caribbean. They also brought cattle and horses.

During the first two decades of the sixteenth century, the Spaniards colonized not only Española, but Cuba, Puerto Rico, and Jamaica as well. They explored the northern coast of South America and founded colonies in Colombia and Panama, but, although they visited many of the islands of the Lesser Antilles, they neither colonized them at this period nor later. In the beginning there were more valuable lands to investigate. The Lesser Antilles were, for the most part, small and were inhabited by the Caribs, who were far better able to defend themselves

than the peaceable Arawaks. Nor is it likely that the Spaniards
foresaw the strategic necessity of occupying these islands to
prevent the encroachment of other European powers. A century later, when the wisdom of this course became obvious,
they were unable to do so.

When on April 22, 1519, Hernando Cortez landed in Mexico
on the site of present-day Vera Cruz, a new epoch in Caribbean
history began, for the tales of wealth which he brought back to
Española resulted in an exodus from the islands to the continent.

The decimation of the Indian population of Española and
the surrounding islands was a result of the brutal methods used
in that day. The consequent labor problems had to be met if the
Spaniards were to benefit from their newly acquired colonies.
The first Negro slaves, which had been purchased or bred in
Spain, were brought to Española by Nicolas de Ovando, the
Governor, in 1502, and in the ensuing years their numbers increased so rapidly that, a short time after the exodus caused by
Cortez's discoveries began, the disparity between blacks and
whites became so great as to alarm the colonists who remained;
and as though to prove that their fears were not unfounded, a
slave uprising occurred in Puerto Rico in 1527.

Within a few years of the discovery of the wealth of Mexico,
other Spaniards ranging along the western coast of South America conquered Peru, and another seemingly endless stream of
gold and silver found its way back to the Spanish treasury. But
Spain was not long allowed undisputed possession of such vast
sources of wealth. Already in 1536, during a period of active
warfare between France and Spain, French privateers had attacked Spanish shipping in the Caribbean, and although these
attacks ended two years later with the Truce of Nice, the Spaniards became so alarmed that they passed the first of several
ordinances requiring all Spanish ships to sail in one of two semi-
annual convoyed fleets for protection.

The Portuguese were the first consistently to ignore Spanish warnings to stay away from the Caribbean, and in the second half of the sixteenth century, they were followed by the French, whose vessels traded with the Spanish colonies in spite of ordinances to the contrary. Nor were the English long to be denied their part in this rich trade. In 1563 and 1565 John Hawkins made two successful voyages to the Caribbean with goods and slaves, but his third voyage in 1568 ended disastrously, when he was forced to take refuge in the Mexican harbor of San Juan de Ulua, after being battered by a tropical storm. Unfortunately, the annual Spanish treasure *flota* arrived two days later, and although the Spaniards agreed to allow Hawkins to repair his ships and to buy food, they treacherously attacked him, and he was fortunate to escape with three of his six ships and scarcely half of his men, many of whom perished on the return voyage. This bit of faithlessness so angered the English that Sir Francis Drake, with a well-equipped privateering squadron, was dispatched the following year to harass the Spaniards in the Caribbean. During the next few years he captured a Spanish treasure convoy on the Isthmus of Panama and sacked Santo Domingo and Cartagena. Meanwhile, the Dutch, who had in 1568 embarked on an eighty years' war with Spain, harassed Spanish shipping in the English Channel and the Bay of Biscay; yet, so great was Spain's power even at this time, that she was able to conquer Portugal in the midst of wars with the Dutch and English.

The early years of the seventeenth century marked attempts at colonization in Guiana by the three leading contenders for Spain's place in the Caribbean—England, France, and Holland; but serious European colonization in the Lesser Antilles did not begin until 1625. Less than two decades later, the white population of these islands had reached the astonishing total of 100,000.

Thus, the other European nations entered the Caribbean by the back door that the Spaniards had so obligingly left open—and in such numbers that they could not be expelled.

This European mass migration was to change the picture of the Caribbean forever. To the aboriginal Indians and the mestizos of European and Indian blood there had been added Negro slaves, a few Moors, natives of Madagascar, and a number of Indian slaves from Massachusetts and Carolina. Now the riffraff of Europe poured into the eastern Caribbean: adventurers, indentured servants recruited from among the unemployed and starving English laboring classes, deserters from the crews of privateers, maroons, laborers from Madeira and the Azores, and German artisans. To these were added Italian mercenaries from the employ of Spain, upper-class Englishmen lured by the prospects of wealth from sugar, and men from New England eager to exchange the inhospitable north for a fortune in the south.

The Caribbean at this time was a melting pot that was ready to boil over. There were many people for whom there was no employment, and there was always a large floating population pursuing wealth or fleeing from starvation. Many indentured servants and deserters joined escaped Negro slaves, maroons, and convicts from English penal colonies to form piratical bands that were later to ravage peaceful settlements and do so much to retard the development of these islands.

It is against this dramatic background of plunder and peaceful colonization, of untold wealth and shocking poverty, of slavery and every form of bondage, of daring exploits, and above all, of the search for wealth, whether from gold or sugar or trade, that the astute Dutch merchants built up a commercial ascendancy which was to last for more than a century. Since the year 1586, Dutch ships had been coming to the West Indies in increasing numbers with slaves and with European-manufactured

British Indian Plantation Worker, Coronie.

Boere Grandmother. .

Atoedendoe, Granman of the Saramaccaner Bush Negroes.

Bauxite Ship on the Cottica River.

Bauxite Plant, Moengo.

Gravenstraat, Paramaribo.

River Defense.

Machine Gunner.

Soesa Dance at Coronie.

Javanese Dance at Groningen.

Bush Negro Boatmen.

Fighting the Rapids on the Surinam River.

Portage at Mamadam.

"Mud Horse" at Coronie.   Three-toed Sloth.

Kotta Missie.

Carib Indian Child.

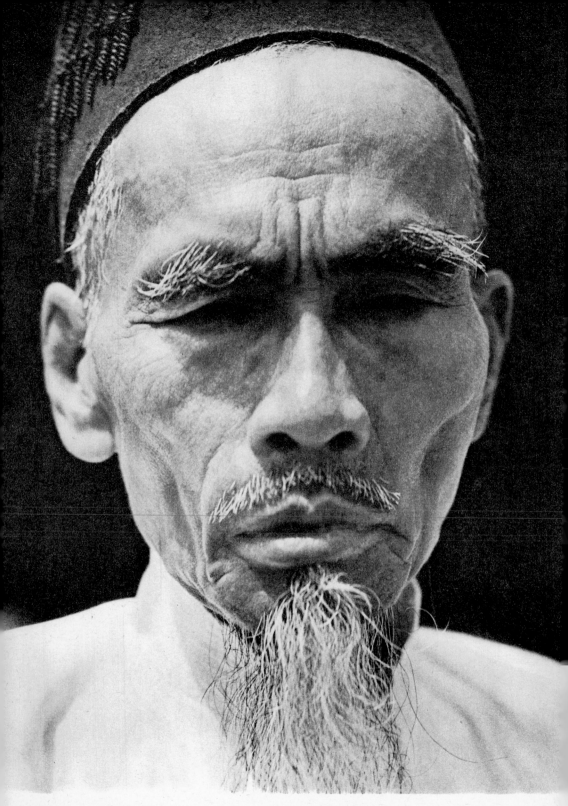

Mohammedan Priest.

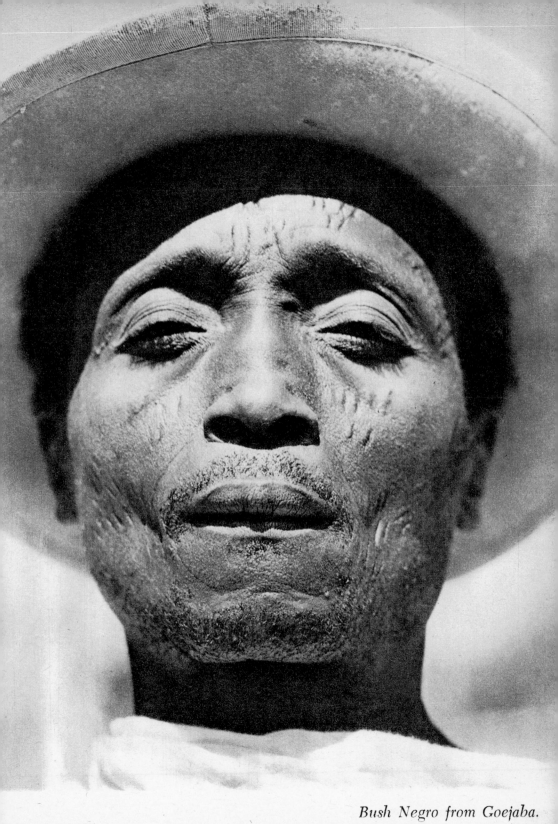

Bush Negro from Goejaba.

Bush Negro Girl.

goods to exchange for hides and dyewood, which at that time were the most important products of the Caribbean.

By 1640 the colonists of the Lesser Antilles began to see the huge profits that could be made from sugar. This had two immediate effects: (1) the discovery that white labor was unsuited to the cultivation of sugar in the tropics, a fact which became apparent when thousands of unfortunate indentured workers sent out from England died on the plantations; (2) a corollary of the first—the greatly increased demand for African slave labor. To the good fortune of the Dutch, this demand came at a time when, due to their long war with Spain, they had built up a very considerable navy and merchant fleet, and at a time when the Portuguese were at war with Spain. The Dutch, furthermore, were in possession of most of the Portuguese slave factories in Africa and had established a near-monopoly in the slave trade. Dutch success, however, cannot be laid entirely to coincidence or good fortune.

The Dutch had from the beginning pursued the policy of becoming middlemen in both merchandise and slaves, rather than colonizers. The English and the French, who attempted to do both, necessarily were less successful in the former. As a consequence, the vast majority of European goods and American produce was carried in Dutch bottoms, and no amount of Spanish blustering, British ordinances, or French demands could prevent this, for the colonists rightly refused to abide by the ordinances of governments in Europe that were interested in the West Indies colonies only for the money they could get out of them and who, furthermore, were unable to supply their needs. This was particularly true of slaves, where the absurdity of the prohibition was so evident as to be ridiculous.

The Spaniards first had granted a monopoly to the Portuguese, but in 1640, when Portugal revolted against Spain, this Portuguese monopoly was withdrawn, and it was not until 1663 that a new *asiento* was granted to an Italian firm, wherein a stipulated number of slaves was to be supplied within a given time. But, as the Dutch held almost absolute control of the trade, it was far easier to buy the slaves at Curaçao and to deliver them to the Spanish colonies from there rather than to import them from Africa. Spanish protests against this practice were unavailing.

Fundamental differences existed between the Spaniards, Dutch, French, and English in the Caribbean. The primary aim of the Spaniards in the New World had been to exploit the mineral resources and to plunder, the Dutch hoped to extend their trade, and many of the English and the French had left Europe with the hope of bettering their economic conditions, of establishing homes, and of enjoying a new freedom from class prejudice and religious intolerance.

Whereas to the Spaniards propagation of the Catholic faith was second in importance only to conquest, it was of little account in the aims of the other nations. The few English attempts to extend Protestantism were soon renounced for more material benefits. The Spaniard differed from the Englishman in another way: whereas the Englishman brought his wife, raised a family, and made a home, the Spaniard took up with the Indian and Negro women.

The Englishman and, to a lesser degree, the Dutchman tended to create as wide a division as possible between himself and his slaves, but the promiscuity of the Spaniard created new racial groups which were accepted as part of the social order. The final disappearance of the Indian population was due to absorption.

Although the state of Caribbean affairs was affected greatly by what was happening in Europe, the dictum "no peace beyond the line" was an acknowledged policy of the European nations, and an act of war or piracy committed in the Indies did not necessarily lead to warfare between the nations in Europe.

The use of privateers as an instrument of national policy began early in the sixteenth century. It was an interesting device for legally harassing an enemy without expense to the national treasury. Letters of marque or reprisal were granted originally to individuals who had suffered loss at the hands of a foreign army or navy, and they were granted only after a petition made to the monarch of that country for indemnity had been refused. Proof had to be submitted that the loss was real and indemnity justified. Later, however, letters of marque were issued indiscriminately on the flimsiest pretext, or on no pretext at all.

Toward the end of the sixteenth century privateering tended to die out, for Spanish ships were heavily convoyed and the practice became too dangerous, but in the early seventeenth century a new source came into being, from which the European nations could assemble privateering squadrons on a scale hitherto not attempted. These were the bands of outlaws—so-called "cow-killers" or buccaneers—named from the *boucan,* a grid over which they broiled their beef or hogs. They lived along the uninhabited coasts and foothills of the larger islands and killed the cattle which were raised by the Spaniards for their hides. The bands were composed of adventurers and the residue of the great influx of white men into the Lesser Antilles. They were desperate men with a past and no future, who were pursued relentlessly by the Spaniards whom they had robbed, and who were treated with the greatest cruelty when they were caught. These men were now employed by the English and the French to prey upon the shipping of other nations. But after several decades during which the policy of their use as a substitute for a regular navy was hotly debated by the Governments of both France and England, it was recognized that such self-interested and undisciplined men could never be depended upon to accomplish national ends; and by the end of the seventeenth century privateering, which by this time had degenerated into downright piracy, was suppressed by both nations.

5

Island Entrepôts

Holland, at the end of the six-
teenth century, needed an outlet for the trade made possible by
her growing naval strength. It also became necessary to find a
new source of salt for her herring industry. It was the latter
which first brought Dutch seamen to the Caribbean Sea and to
the shores of South America, for after the defeat of Portugal by
Spain in 1580, the Portuguese salt pans were closed to the Dutch.

Until 1621 Dutch trade with the Americas was carried on by
individual merchants. But in 1610 Hendrik Hudson, in the employ of the Dutch East India Company, had explored the coast
of North America and, as a result, a trading station and fort
were built on Manhattan Island. This fort was destroyed by the
English, but it was rebuilt the following year, and a charter was
granted to the Company of New Netherland, giving them exclusive rights to exploit the country from Chesapeake Bay to Newfoundland. Actual colonization of New Netherland was confined to the country between the English colonies of New England and Virginia, and this Dutch settlement was a thorn in the
side of the British for fifty years.

The success of the Dutch East India Company brought about
a demand in Holland that a similar company he formed to exploit the Western Hemisphere and thus avoid competition
among Dutch merchants. It was thought that in this way greater

benefits would be realized by the Netherlands as a whole. A Dutch West India Company was therefore granted a charter by the States General on June 3, 1621. The West India Company was to be governed by nineteen representatives, "The Nineteen," and it received a monopoly for twenty-four years of navigation and trade on the east coast of Africa between twenty-three and one-half degrees north and twenty-three and one-half degrees south of the equator, and of all lands lying between the south coast of Newfoundland and the Straits of Magellan. The aims of the company, in keeping with the times, were those of conquest and buccaneering rather than the peaceful pursuit of trade.

By the terms of its charter the West India Company was granted virtually all the rights of sovereignty—the right to declare war, to acquire possessions and to make treaties; and the territory embraced by the charter gave the company control of the slave trade. In addition, the States General undertook to supply sixteen warships and four auxiliary ships on the condition that the Company would supply the same number. It was also incumbent upon the States General to supply troops, though at the Company's expense. The States General subsidized the Dutch West India Company to the extent of one million guilders, but dividends were to be paid on only half of this amount. The Company further was granted freedom of imports and exports.

The newly constituted Dutch West India Company immediately set about an ambitious program of conquest and colonization. At first a profitable trade was carried on with the Negroes and Indians and also with the Spanish colonists. But the prospects of buccaneering seemed even more attractive, particularly after the Company's admiral, Piet Hein, with a fleet of thirty-one ships, surprised the Spanish treasure *flota* at Matanzas Bay and took an enormous booty of gold, silver, hides, indigo, cochineal, sugar, and precious stones, which brought a profit to the Company of nearly twelve million guilders. This success, however, was incorrectly interpreted by the directors, who immediately declared a dividend of fifty per cent, whereas the Company was able to pay only an average dividend of two per cent thereafter.

The success of Admiral Hein and the capture of the Spanish silver fleet in 1629 induced the Company to begin operations on a large scale in Brazil, and in 1634 an expedition under Johannes van Welbeck occupied Curaçao and the neighboring islands of Aruba and Bonaire without opposition from the Spaniards. Between 1616 and 1648 Guiana and the islands of St. Eustatius, Saba, and St. Martin were colonized by other Dutchmen, principally from Zeeland, and the Dutch West India Company also strengthened its position in New Netherland. By 1642 its possessions extended from New Netherland to Brazil, and it virtually controlled the lucrative slave and carrying trades.

Following its initial success, the West India Company experienced a series of difficulties. The revolt of Portugal from Spanish rule in 1640 held out the promise of a new ally in the war against Spain, but the Dutch East and West India Companies had both profited at Portugal's expense during the sixty years of its subjection, and it was soon realized that Portuguese friendship could be bought only at the expense of a restitution of all conquests.

In 1641 a treaty of non-aggression was made with Portugal, and this severely handicapped the Dutch West India Company by preventing acts of piracy against Portuguese shipping—a large source of the Company's revenues. The Company finances also suffered from the heavy expenses of maintaining a large fleet and garrisoning the various settlements. A program of economy, therefore, was begun in Brazil, in spite of the fact that the

Brazilians, secretly helped by the Portuguese, had already revolted. Several defeats in Brazil finally resulted in a withdrawal from that country in 1654.

Following this disaster, the colony of New Netherland was seized by the British without a declaration of war, and although it was retaken by the Dutch, it was captured by the British during the second Anglo-Dutch war. Surinam was captured during the same war by the Dutch captain, Abraham Crijnssen, who had been sent out by the Province of Zeeland, and at the Treaty of Breda in 1667 the English were confirmed in their possession of New Netherland, whereas the Dutch retained Surinam. This solution was of advantage to both nations, for it consolidated the British colonies in North America and the Dutch colonies in Guiana. The Dutch West India Company, however, suffered the loss of New Netherland, whereas Surinam did not come into its possession until 1682.

The Company, now in severe financial straits, attempted to merge with the East India Company in an effort to offset its losses by profits in the East, and although this was not effected, it did receive a subsidy of one million five hundred thousand guilders from the East India Company. All efforts to prop the West India Company's tottering finances were unavailing, however, and on December 31, 1674, it was dissolved at the expiration of its license.

A second West India Company, with a more limited charter than that of the first company, was immediately established. With the exception of the year 1720, when it paid a dividend of one hundred and fifty per cent, this company was never especially successful. It continued in existence until 1791, when it, too, was dissolved and the colonies came under the jurisdiction of the States General.

Curaçao must have been well known to the Dutch a century

or more before its conquest by the West India Company, for since its discovery on July 26, 1499, by an expedition led by Alonzo de Ojeda, reports had been drifting back to Europe, many of which were less fanciful than the description of Amerigo Vespucci, who had been a member of Ojeda's party.

Vespucci's account, though it is of questionable authenticity, neverthelesss is interesting.

We found [afterwards] that a race of very great stature dwelt therein: we then landed to see if we found [could find] fresh water: and imagining that the island was not inhabited because we saw no people, going along the shore we beheld very large footsteps of men on the sand: and we judged, if their other members were of corresponding size, that they must be very big men: and proceeding onwards, we came upon a pathway which led to the interior of the land: and nine of us agreed: and concluded that the island being small could not contain within itself many people: and thereupon we went onward through it, to see what manner of people they were: and after we had gone for about a league, we beheld in a valley five of their huts, which appeared uninhabited: and we made our way to them and found only five women, two old ones and three girls, so lofty in stature that we gazed at them in astonishment: and when they saw us, so much terror overcame them that they had not even spirit to flee away: and the two old women began to invite us with words, bringing us many things to eat, and they put us in a hut: and they were in stature taller than a tall man, so that they would be quite as big of body as was Francesco degli Albizi, but better proportioned: so much that we were all of a mind to take away the three girls from them by force: and to carry them to Castile as a prodigy: and while thus discussing, there began to enter through the door of the hut full 36 men much bigger than the women: more so well built that it was a famous sight to see them: who put us in such uneasiness that we would much rather have been in our ships than in the company of such people. They carried very large bows and arrows, with large knobbed clubs: and they spoke among themselves in such a tone as though they meant to lay hands upon us; seeing that we were in such danger, we debated of various plans among ourselves: some [of us] said that we ought to attack immediately in the house: and others that it were better on the open ground [outside]: and others who said that we ought not to begin the quarrel until we should see what they meant to do: and we agreed to go further from the hut and to make our way slily towards the ships: and so we did: and having taken our way we returned to the ships: those [savages] however came following behind us, always at a distance of a stone's throw, speaking amongst themselves: I believe that they were no less afraid of us than we were of them: because we halted sometimes, and they did the same without approaching nearer until we reached the shore where the boats were awaiting us: and we entered into them: and when we were at some distance, they danced about and shot many arrows at us: but we had little dread of them now: we fired two gunshots at them, more to terrify them than to do any hurt: and at the explosion they all fled inwards: and so we departed from them, having as it seemed to us escaped from a perilous day's work. They went entirely naked like the others. I call that island, the Isle of Giants, because of their great size: and we proceeded onward still skirting the coast on which it befel us many times to have to fight them, as they sought not to allow us to take anything from the land.

As to the name Curaçao, there is certainly no justification for the story that the Spanish *Curazzo* is derived from *cura hasado*, or roasted priest. More likely it has been taken from the Indian name for the island—*coaracy, curassi sun,* or *quaraci.*

Curaçao was first colonized by the Spaniards in 1527, and the islands of Aruba and Bonaire were occupied during the following two years. They were placed under the Governor of Coro in Venezuela. In 1565 the island was described by Hawkins as "one great cattle ranch," and although the Spaniards occupied it for more than a century, there are no indications that they did much toward developing it. The cattle were allowed to run wild on the island, and it is probable that many trees were cut down at this time to allow for grazing.

The Spaniards cannot have considered Curaçao to have been of much importance, for they did not defend it, and the garrison was unable to oppose the expedition of Johannes van Welbeck in 1634, and surrendered on the condition that it be transported to the coast of Venezuela with its goods and slaves. Some accounts maintain that the entire Indian population of Curaçao was transported to the continent; others that seventy-five Indians were allowed to remain. If the latter is true, they were completely absorbed by the growing European and African population, for today no trace of them remains; whereas, on the islands of Aruba and Bonaire, Indian ancestry is still evident among the population.

Accounts of the indigenes are conflicting, as few explorers of the time were competent observers, and the account of a sixteenth-century writer differs widely from the version of Amerigo Vespucci. The former describes them as being "of meek and soft character, and inclined to Christianity."

Archeological research has given more positive information as to the nature of the Indian civilization. The most interesting Indian remains on the Dutch islands are the pictographs in the caves at Onima and Spelonk on the island of Bonaire. The largest cave is at Spelonk, where Father Brenneker, a Catholic priest who has taken an interest in the subject, has counted three hundred and five drawings. There are four more caves near Onima and two others near by. In one of the caves at Onima the drawings are particularly clear and are painted in red on a brilliant yellow background. Red paint is used throughout the other caves, with a single exception, where a combination of black and red paint is employed. In a few instances the drawings have been scratched into the rock, rather than painted.

In some of the drawings rays are drawn from natural holes in the surface of the rock. These may represent suns, but they may be merely decorations, though if this is the case, it is strange that many of the finest surfaces have not been used. It has been suggested that these pictographs have religious significance or that they are esoteric family or clan symbols. By the use of a little imagination one can read a crab or a snake or a fish into some of the drawings. Others are more abstract and consist of concentric circles, crosses within crosses, or parallel lines or combinations of dots and lines. It is possible to imagine sexual symbolism in a few of the figures, yet there is no real indication that this was the intention, and speculation as to their true meaning has so far been fruitless.

A few pictographs are also to be found on the islands of Curaçao and Aruba, though the former may be recent imitations.

The pottery found on Bonaire and usually attributed to the Indians is coarse and made of inferior clay. It more closely resembles Negro pottery to be found in many of the Caribbean islands, but the pieces that I saw were all extremely fragmentary, and it was impossible to form a true opinion.

Stone axes, so common to the West Indian islands and South America, are also to be found in Bonaire. Many of them are of a stone not found on the island, and the present-day Negro population shares the Caribbean superstition that they are dashed to earth during thunderstorms. On Bonaire they are called *piedra di boz, piedra di hacha,* or *hacha di strena*—literally thunderstone, thunderaxe or lightning axe.

Superstitions regarding thunderstones are similar to those encountered throughout the West Indies. One is that a genuine thunderstone, placed on the windowsill, is a guarantee against lightning striking the house. To discover if a stone is genuine, a cord is tied tightly around it and the stone is then placed in a fire. If the ends of the cord burn and the part touching the stone remains intact, then the stone is genuine and becomes quite valuable.

A local explanation of why most thunderstones are found in a damaged condition with the blade edge nicked or dulled is that, as the stones are dashed to earth with great violence during storms, it is only natural that they should be chipped.

The Dutch, by their conquest of Curaçao, came into possession of an island with several excellent harbors which were to serve them well in their efforts to harass Spanish shipping. As an entrepôt of trade for both the northern coast of Venezuela and for the rich island of Española, it became the transshipment port for great quantities of sugar, indigo, cocoa, and tobacco. The island was strongly fortified and large warehouses and slave pens were built, and although the prosperity of Curaçao was based on trade, the island supported a limited amount of agriculture; sugar, tobacco, oranges, cotton, millet, and indigo were raised on its plantations.

William Dampier, in *A New Voyage Around the World*, written at the close of the seventeenth century, described Curaçao in the following words:

At the East end are two hills, one of them is much higher than the other, and steepest toward the North side. The rest of the Island is indifferent level; where of late some rich Men have made Sugar works; which formerly was all pasture for Cattle: there are also some small Plantations of Potatoes and Yames, and they have still a great many Cattle on the Island; but it is not so much esteemed for its produce, as for its situation for the Trade with the Spaniard. Formerly the Harbour was never without Ships from Cartagene and Portabell, that did use to buy of the Dutch here 1000 or 1500 Negroes at once, besides great quantities of European Commodities; but of late that Trade is fallen into the hands of the English at Jamaica: yet still the Dutch have a vast Trade over all the West-Indies, sending from Holland Ships of good force laden with European goods, whereby they make very profitable returns. The Dutch have two other Islands here, but of little moment in comparison of Querisao; the one lieth 7 or 8 leagues to the Westward of Querisao, called Aruba; the other 9 or 10 leagues to the Eastward of it, called Bon-Airy. From these Islands the Dutch fetch in sloops Provision for Querisao, to maintain their Garrison and Negroes.

Much of the early prosperity of Curaçao was due to the Portuguese Jews, experienced agriculturists from Brazil, who were permitted to immigrate on the condition that they continue to engage in agriculture. The first Jew known to have come to Curaçao was Samuel Coheño, a Portuguese employed as interpreter, who arrived with the Dutch expedition which conquered Curaçao in 1634. He remained on the island as an interpreter to deal with the Indians. The earliest group of Portuguese Jews arrived in Curaçao in 1651 under a charter granted to Joáo Ilháo, and in the following year a second group of so-called sephardic Jews, or *marranos*, was brought by another Portuguese Jew, Joseph Nunes da Fonseca, alias David Nassi. The privileges granted to Nassi were embodied in a remarkably liberal charter, the first in which the Jews in the New World were granted freedom of religion.

The Jewish congregation, Mikvé Israel, was founded in 1656, and a building on the plantation *De Hoop* was used for the original synagogue. This plantation was situated on the northwestern side of the Schottegat close to the present Jewish cemetery, which has graves dating back to 1656.

The Jewish colony was further enlarged in 1654 by the arrival of other Portuguese Jews who had fled from Brazil, and one of them, Geosuah de Mordechay Henriquez, was instrumental in bringing twelve more Jewish families—about seventy persons in all—to Curaçao from Holland in 1659 to form an agrarian colony under a charter granted to Isaac da Costa. Many of these Jews did not engage in agriculture; instead, they founded the trading companies and business houses, which have been perpetuated to the present time. The names "Henriquez" and "da Costa" are still well known, and "Maduro," a later addition, is so common that it is almost impossible to go anywhere in Curaçao without meeting someone by that name. An official told me that, when he first came to Curaçao, he had met a great many people in a short time and had had great difficulty in remembering all of their names. "I solved the problem very well," he said, "by calling everyone that I met 'Mr. Maduro,' which gave me a better than even chance of being right."

In 1692 a synagogue was built in Willemstad on the Joode Kerckstraat, and its first rabbi was the famous Josiao Pardo, who later became rabbi of the synagogue in Kingston, Jamaica. The Willemstad synagogue was built in 1732, when the Jewish population had grown to two thousand. It is a replica of the synagogue in Amsterdam, and it is the oldest one in the Western Hemisphere.

The Jewish population, which was both wealthy and powerful, played a leading role in establishing Curaçao's economic position, but subsequently several families left the island, and the colony dwindled, until today it numbers only 735. It has, however, continued to maintain its wealth and influence and social position.

In the seventeenth and eighteenth centuries the West Indian colonies became the richest in the world, and immense fortunes were made from slave-grown sugar. The West Indian islands were not only easily accessible to Europe because sailing vessels were almost always assured of a favorable wind in both directions—the trade winds carrying them across, and the southwesterlies back—but they provided a large outlet for European-manufactured goods, whereas the East Indies were not only inaccessible, but their commodities had to be paid for in cash, so that a profit was made only on the return voyage. Africa was no market at all, and neither North America nor South America was at that time sufficiently developed. Even at the end of the eighteenth century the Caribbean colonies were considered to be of more value than those in North America.

Curaçao prospered because it was so well defended that it was not attacked by every privateer or buccaneer who sailed past the island, and who was the curse of so many other Caribbean outposts. Its greatest difficulties, in fact, arose from internal friction between the governor appointed by the West India Company and his assistants, all of whom were grossly underpaid and who frequently resorted to graft at the expense of company interests.

With the entrance of the English, French, and Dutch into the Caribbean scene, sugar became the principal product of the West Indies. The small islands of the Lesser Antilles were preferred because they could be more easily protected by the fleets of the various nations, because the difficulties of transportation to the coast were lessened, and because the slaves which were brought in increasing numbers could be more easily controlled.

St. Martin, Saba, and St. Eustatius were probably either sighted by Columbus on his second voyage, or discovered shortly thereafter, for the prevailing winds from Europe brought the sailing ships to the West Indies in their neighborhood. But it is improbable that the present island of St. Martin is the one so named by Columbus. Historians recently have concluded that the St. Martin of Columbus is more likely the island of Nevis, though descriptions of his voyage and contemporary maps leave much to the imagination.

The Lesser Antilles at the time of their discovery were inhabited by the Caribs, but accounts differ as to whether there was any permanent Indian population on the islands of St. Martin, St. Eustatius, and Saba. The Caribs are known to have moved from island to island, which partly accounts for these conflicting reports. Another reason that their permanent occupation by the Indians is doubtful was the scarcity of water.

The first French and English colonists that came to St. Eustatius in 1625 and in 1629 left due to the lack of water, and it was not until 1632 that the island was permanently colonized by a party of Zeelanders, who built wells and cisterns similar to those in use today.

The early history of Saba is obscure. The island is variously believed to have been settled by Zeelanders, Scotch Presbyterians, and Irishmen, but the last hypothesis is extremely doubtful, for in the beginning of the nineteenth century, there were no Catholics on the island. Most likely the first settlers were Zeelanders who came from Europe in 1640.

Names now common on the island, such as Simonsz, Zeegers, and Heyliger support this theory, though the first two have been Anglicized to Simmons and Sagors. These names are also common to Flushing and Middleburg.

Dutch salt workers are known to have occupied the island of St. Martin by 1631, but there is an even earlier account of a hurricane in 1623 which destroyed the shipping in the roadstead. In 1633 the Spaniards drove out the Dutch salt workers, but by 1640 they abandoned the island to the Dutch and the French, who settled permanently in 1648.

There is an apocryphal story which describes the manner of the original division of the island. A Dutchman and a Frenchman agreed to start walking in opposite directions from a point on the eastern side of the island, and a dividing line was to be drawn from the starting place to where they met. It was a long walk, and the Frenchman took wine with him for refreshment, and the Dutchman took beer. The beer was heavier than the wine, and the Dutchman was fatter than the Frenchman; consequently, the Dutch received the smaller portion of the island. But the Dutchman was the more astute, for he started walking around the southern part of the island, which is the richer. More sober accounts, while not denying this story, describe the signing of a treaty between the Dutch and the French on March 26, 1648, on the top of Mont des Accords, from which a large part of the island can be seen. This treaty, dividing the land and the natural resources of St. Martin and concluding an offensive and defensive alliance, remained in effect until 1839, when it was replaced by a new treaty.

These three small Dutch islands are of far less importance than the surrounding British and French ones. This is due in part to the fact that at the time of their conquest the Dutch West India Company was enmeshed in a war in Brazil and wished to avoid further conflict, and in part to the Dutch policy of securing bases for trade, rather than colonies. Neither St. Eustatius nor Saba has a harbor, or even a good roadstead, and though Great Bay in St. Martin is protected, its value to the Dutch as a port was lessened by the fact that the island was half French. St. Thomas, with its magnificent harbor, was not at that time in the possession of any European power, but it was too close to the Spaniards in Puerto Rico to guarantee immunity from attack.

The history of Saba from the beginning was bound up with that of St. Eustatius, and for the first one hundred and fifty years it was administered by a Vice-Commander, under the Commander of St. Eustatius. Saba never had any commercial value in the eyes of the European nations competing for supremacy in the Lesser Antilles, due to its precipitous slopes, which were unsuitable to large-scale agriculture, and because of its inaccessibility from the sea. Nevertheless, it was several times plundered by buccaneers and changed hands frequently with the rise and fall of Dutch, English, and French fortunes. In the latter part of the seventeenth century its population was predominantly English, and as much of its trade, as well as that of St. Eustatius and St. Martin, was carried on with the adjacent English-speaking islands, it is not strange that English, rather than Dutch, has become its language.

St. Martin and St. Eustatius were planted with sugar and later with cotton, but as little attention was paid to soil conservation and since the forests of these islands were destroyed, much of the best soil has been blown away or washed into the sea, leaving the land good only for grazing.

St. Eustatius, however, was valuable to the Dutch as an outlet for trade, not agriculture, and the Dutch West India Company fortified the island and then set about creating a smaller image of Curaçao to serve as an entrepôt for North America and Central America and the islands of the Lesser Antilles. Several hundred slaves were always kept on the island, just as manufactured goods from Europe were stocked in the warehouses to be exchanged for the sugar, tobacco, cotton, indigo, dyewood, hides, and cochineal of the Western Hemisphere.

Only three decades after the establishment of the Dutch in Curaçao and St. Eustatius, British and French jealousy of Dutch control of the slave trade and the carrying trade resulted in the declaration of open warfare between the three countries. During the next two hundred years the fortunes of St. Martin, Saba, and St. Eustatius fluctuated with every whim of European diplomacy, and the islands suffered numerous times from privateers and buccaneers. Between 1664 and 1674, for example, St. Eustatius changed hands ten times, being successively captured by the English and the French and sacked by buccaneers. For fourteen of the twenty-two years from 1674 to 1696 the island was occupied by the English.

The period of Dutch commercial ascendancy is not particularly well defined, though it falls roughly between 1586 and 1678, with a peak about 1642. It is overlapped, however, at one end by the waning but by no means negligible power of the Spaniards, and on the other by the increasing might of the English.

The successive Anglo-Dutch wars broke the links between the English and French planters and the Dutch merchants, and when the Dutch lines of communication were finally cut at both ends by the French privateers in 1678, France and England were left in possession of the seas and consequently of the West Indies trade.

At the close of the seventeenth century, Holland, France, and England renounced the use of privateering fleets, and a more orderly, though scarcely more peaceful, period ensued. Warfare was now carried on by navies, rather than by undisciplined cutthroats, and the Caribbean was brought within the bounds of international comity. No longer was it possible to commit acts of piracy without suffering their consequences.

A period of Anglo-French rivalry for the carrying trade, extending throughout the eighteenth century, resulted from Holland's eclipse; but France had been profligate with her power and was exhausted by a series of long wars, and England gradually became the dominant power in the Caribbean, though she achieved no clear-cut victory over France for many years. Holland, moreover, was a significant competitor for Caribbean trade.

The period of turmoil in Europe gradually came to a close and a period of comparative peace ensued, which was reflected in the Caribbean and which was not to be broken until the American Revolution. With peace came prosperity, and at last the planters were assured of the fruits of their labors. For a few years the fears of pillage and ransom could be set aside.

6

The Rise of Surinam

THE history of Guiana dates back to within a decade of the discovery of the New World. The first reports refer to it as the "Wild Coast," and the tales which reached Europe were lurid enough to merit the name. They told of Eldorado and of mermaids, headless men, and Amazons.

Surinam was the original home of the Arawaks, the most civilized of the Guiana Indians. They were peaceful agriculturists and proficient workers in stone. The Caribs, though originating in the middle of South America, at an early time moved to the Guianas and to the territory adjacent to the lower Orinoco River. They were fierce head-hunters and cannibals and became the traditional enemies of the Arawaks.

The Kalina-Galibi, or lowland Caribs, and the Arawaks lived on the alluvial coastal plain on the sand and shell ridges raised above the level of high tide, and it is here that stone celts and burial urns filled with human bones are still found.

The ordinary Surinam celt is of the petaloid type common to the West Indies, while others have square or concave butts, and the majority are notched so that they can be lashed to wooden handles. A very fine celt, shown to me by Commissioner Hagen at Nieuw Amsterdam, was carved with the head of a capybara, the largest quadruped rodent in the world, which looks like a huge guinea pig and is native to the rivers of South America. The carving showed high artistic achievement, as well as considerable competency in stone work.

The Arawaks numbering 1,100 and the Caribs 1,000 together form about four-fifths of the present Indian population of Surinam. There are also about 100 Wamas living on the Corantijn River along the border of British Guiana. Close to the Brazilian border, at the headwaters of the Paloemeu and Litani Rivers, there are 226 Trios, 170 Oajanas, and 20 Wamas.

The Trios and the Oajanas were very carefully counted in 1941 and 1942 by Loedwijk Schmidt, a Bush Negro from Gansee who is the watchman for the Government Agricultural Experiment Station. He also found 460 Trios and 170 Oajanas on the Brazilian side of the border.

The mortality among the Oajanas evidently has been very high, for only thirty-five years ago they were estimated at 1,000, a decrease of about two per cent a year.

The Wamas are an entirely wild tribe, living in the Oranje Mountains between the headwaters of the Tapanahoni and Litani Rivers. They have no agriculture and exist by hunting and from the tubers of wild plants. All of these Indians live in small villages numbering from fifteen to forty persons, and move every three to five years, when the soil of their provision grounds has become exhausted. This has proved very confusing to mapmakers, for not only the location, but the name of the village, is changed.

The Oajanas and the Trios live in the jungle, not on the savanna, the former along the rivers, the latter on the small creeks hidden by overhanging trees.

The entire southeastern section of Surinam is uninhabited, so far as is known, and the possibility that there may be tribes hidden in the mountains and small unexplored rivers is remote, as most of this country has been reconnoitered from the air.

Tales of white Indians in the South American jungles have been as common in the past few decades as those of Amazons in the sixteenth century, but five years ago some point was given to these stories when an Indian woman was brought to Paramaribo by a Moravian missionary from the upper Marowijne River. She came from a tribe that had been called Ojarikoele, but to which she gave the name of Triometesem. The existence of this tribe had been established previously by explorers, who had heard of it from Indians on the Tapanahoni River. It is known to have had a stone-age culture and to have been extremely savage and hostile. This Indian woman has been described as "light skinned, with green eyes, hair straight and brownish and cut in a fringe. Her figure rather square—a shy creature." It is possible that she was the last member of her tribe, for an expedition sent out the following year was unable to find any trace of it.

All of the Guiana Indians live in much the same state as they did when the country was first discovered. The tendency of the Indian was to retreat before the advance of civilization. Among white men he lost his identity, but in the jungle he was at home. Warfare with the early settlers had greatly reduced his numbers, and jungle life was changed. The Indian population became so thinly spread that tribal warfare gradually died out; the Carib, who had been a warrior, grew apathetic from a life of idleness; and the Arawak, who no longer had to defend himself from attack, became equally dull and phlegmatic.

The Indian was once a far more experienced boatman and a better hunter than the Bush Negro, but he has lost interest in life. Perhaps he recognizes himself as a member of a dying race

—probably he does not think about it at all. Over a period of years he has done less and less, until now he is capable of doing nothing.

The women have been far less affected by civilization than the men, which is understandable because women's work—agriculture, cooking, and childbearing—have not lost their importance.

The Carib women still wear only short aprons called *queyas*, heavy strings of beads around their necks, and woven cotton bands about their legs just below the knees, and other bands above the ankles. For festive occasions they add a few more beads and wear a cloth which is carried under one arm and tied over the other shoulder. But most of the men in the coastal districts have given up their loincloths for filthy trousers and shirts which are far from picturesque and detrimental to their health. Those in the interior, however, wear traditional dress and have magnificent feather head-dresses for feast days.

All of the Guiana Indians are particularly susceptible to tuberculosis, which has decimated many of the tribes. This is due largely to their eating and drinking habits, for their food is eaten from a common pot. They also drink *piwaree*, which is made by chewing cassava bread and spitting it into a container. Water is added, and after a few days it has fermented and is ready to be drunk. If one Indian in the village has tuberculosis, it is bound to spread to the others.

The Caribs at one time practiced rites of initiation that were designed to test the stamina and fortitude of the young boys before they became members of the tribe. They allowed manourie ants to sting them, and they cut gashes into their chests and arms into which they rubbed the acrid juices of plants. Another test was to pass a long, fine tube greased with the fat of palm caterpillars, narrow at one end and more than a quarter of an inch in diameter at the other end, through the nostril and out of the mouth.

The Oajana Indians still practice similar rites. There is a wasp test that is given to both boys and girls on their initiation into the tribe, and also to older men who have been unsuccessful at hunting. Wasps are taken from their nests early in the morning by using a narcotic prepared from a jungle tree or a palm. The heads of the stupefied wasps are then placed in the wide end of a quill, and the quill is pushed through a mat made of palm straw, so that the opening closes on the thin middle of the wasp and fixes it in place. In this mat 360 wasps of a particularly virulent species are fixed closely together.

As a prelude to the ceremony, the boys put on an *olak*—a head-dress of macaw feathers and the glistening parts of insects —and they dance without interruption until just before the dawn, when the true test begins. They are then divested of their ornaments, and one of the mats, with the awakened and thoroughly angry wasps, is brought out. The boy or girl is supported by two men and the mat is placed first on the chest, then on the back, the arms, the legs—in fact, over the entire body. During the test the initiates are not supposed to display the slightest sign of emotion, in spite of the fact that the pain is so severe and so much poison has been absorbed into the system that they have to remain in their hammocks for a week to recover.

The day following the test a number of the tribesmen, who probably represent evil spirits, break into the hut and shake every hammock to increase the suffering. If this final test is passed without an outcry, then the boy or girl is accepted into the tribe.

The Oajanas also test young girls by allowing ants to sting

them, which is supposed to make them as industrious as the ants.

Such were the aboriginal inhabitants of Guiana that greeted the early explorers.

In 1593 Guiana was claimed by Philip II of Spain, but it was never colonized by the Spaniards, whose treatment of the Indians provoked fierce resistance and who lost interest when their dreams of Eldorado proved to be unfounded.

Sir Walter Raleigh was also disappointed in his expectations of finding gold, but by the end of the sixteenth century the first British, Dutch, and French traders were already coming to Guiana, hoping to make their fortunes from trade and agriculture.

Captain Charles Leigh, an Englishman, founded the first Guiana colony in 1604 on the Oyapock River, which forms the present boundary between French Guiana and Brazil, but it was unsuccessful, and several attempts by the French and English to revive it or to form other settlements were equally unsuccessful.

Two Dutch trading posts were established on the Surinam and the Corantijn Rivers in 1613 in what is now Surinam, but the former was abandoned and the latter was destroyed by the Spaniards. It remained for a Dutchman to establish the first permanent Guiana colony in 1816, when Captain Groenewegen, with a company of Englishmen and Zeelanders, settled on the Essequebo River. British Guiana, therefore, was first colonized by the Dutch and Surinam by the English.

In 1630 Captain Marshall, with sixty Englishmen, settled on the Surinam River to plant tobacco, but this colony had to be abandoned, and a second colony founded by Captain Marshall in 1643 was destroyed by the Indians two years later. These two colonies, however, laid the foundation for the first permanent colony in Surinam, which was founded in 1652 by Lord Willoughby, Earl of Parham, who had previously been made Governor of all the British Caribbean islands.

The name Paramaribo is not derived from the name of its founder, but is of Indian origin.

Willoughby brought with him a number of English Jews who settled on the Jews' Savanna some miles above Paramaribo on the Surinam River.

The archives show that there was a Jewish settlement in 1639, and there are indications that the first Jews may have arrived as early as 1632.

More Jewish colonists came to Surinam under the leadership of David Nassi after the Portuguese reconquest of Brazil, and these Portuguese Jews were granted a charter by the English which was substantially the same as the liberal charter granted to the Jews in Curaçao in 1652. These Jews also settled close to the Jews' Savanna and were instrumental in putting the colony on a sound basis.

Willoughby's colony prospered and was in constant communication with the already well-established British colonies in the Lesser Antilles. But fifteen years after its founding and a year after Lord Willoughby himself had been drowned when most of his fleet was driven ashore during an attack on the French island of Martinique, Surinam was captured by the Dutch under Captain Abraham Crijnssen, who had been commissioned by the Province of Zeeland.

The terms of surrender included an article which later greatly affected the prosperity of the colony. It read: "In case any inhabitant of the colony shall now or hereafter intend to depart hence, he shall have power to sell his estate, and the governor in this case shall procure that he be transported at a moderate freight together with his estate."

The Treaty of Breda ending the Second Anglo-Dutch War was signed on July 31, 1667, but the news did not reach the

West Indies until much later. Meanwhile, Sir John Harman, at
the head of a British fleet, recaptured Surinam and transported
the Dutch garrison to Barbados.

When the terms of the Treaty of Breda were finally made
known, the entire colony was thrown into confusion. The British
Governor at first refused to return Surinam to the Dutch, and
when he saw that he must eventually do so, he decided to strip
it of everything of value. The Dutch were equally anxious to
prevent the departure of the colonists and the removal of their
property. But in 1669 a number of English plantation owners,
together with their Negro slaves—altogether 1,200 people—left
to settle on the island of Jamaica. Included in this number were
200 Jewish colonists.

Other Jews left Surinam in 1675, yet in 1694 there were 574
Jews in Surinam owning more than forty plantations and 9,000
slaves.

Surinam, by Crijnssen's conquest, became the property of
Zeeland. But Zeeland was unable to bear the expense of supplying and defending it, and in 1682, after fifteen years of an indifferent government, the colony was sold to the Dutch West
India Company.

The Dutch West India Company, however, was no more able
to bear the expense than the Province of Zeeland, and a few
months later it sold a one-third interest to the City of Amsterdam and another third to the House of Sommelsdijk. The three
shareholders formed the Chartered Society of Surinam, which,
by a resolution of the States General, was entrusted with the
government of the colony, and Cornelius van Aerssen van Sommelsdijk was persuaded to become Governor without compensation. He came to Paramaribo in 1683 and immediately
established a strong government to deal with the lawless elements which had sprung up in the colony.

Paramaribo at the time of his arrival was guarded by Fort

Zeelandia and is described as a settlement of "only twenty-seven dwellings, more than half of which were grog-shops."

Sommelsdijk's first step was to subdue the Indian tribes which had become an increasing menace to the colony due to raids made in retribution for the enslavement of members of the tribes. The campaign was carried forward vigorously and the Indians were soon ready to accept terms of peace, which assured them their freedom and granted them land. Very little trouble thereafter was experienced in Surinam from the Indians, but there were further uprisings in Berbice and Essequebo, where the planters did not live up to the terms of the agreement respecting slavery. An immediate result of the treaty with the Indians made it possible for the planted areas to be considerably expanded.

Sommelsdijk created a council of administration, a supreme court, and a court of criminal justice. He also encouraged immigration, and during his governorship many French refugee families came to Surinam. Captain Stedman a century later described him as having "the character of a tyrant; he was, under the cloak of religion, despotic, passionate, brutal, and cruel." What he says may be true, but it is equally true that the situation required a person of strong character and some firmness of purpose. Others have called him the real founder of the colony, and Surinam unquestionably benefited from his rule.

Subsequent events somewhat justify Stedman's appraisal, for five years after Sommelsdijk came to Surinam, he was murdered by his own soldiers, who claimed that he had not only forced them to work like slaves in digging canals, but had also given them too little food.

The first colonists settled on the Surinam River at some distance from the sea, for the reasons that much of the coastal alluvium was under water at high tide and also because they were afforded some protection against privateering attacks by their remote location. The fact that this land was not particularly fertile, however, led to the development of the coastal area, where the problems encountered were of a different kind. First, the forests had to be felled and the land cleared. This process and empoldering, which consists of surrounding an area of cleared ground with dikes and draining it by canals with sluice gates that can be opened at low tide, was economically possible only in the days of slavery. Many polders also have navigation and irrigation canals, the former because it was easier to build canals than roads, the latter because Surinam suffered from periodical droughts, in spite of the fact that the rainfall at Paramaribo averages ninety inches a year. This average, however, is subject to marked deviation from year to year, and there is also considerable variation according to locality. J. Warren Nystrom, in *Surinam, a Geographic Study*, notes a climatic cycle in which droughts occur every twelve to fourteen years.

Polders, once built, had to be kept in repair, and the canals kept free of vegetation; and the jungle was always ready to reclaim any plantation that was not being cared for. Only the Dutch, with their wide experience with polders, would have attempted to cultivate this area.

The nature of the topography and the climate limits Surinam's crops to tropical lowland varieties. The temperature averages 79° Fahrenheit, with a variation of 3.4° between the warmest and the coolest months, with a high relative humidity. The land nowhere rises more than a hundred meters above the level of the sea within seventy-five miles of the coast, but this area reaches far beyond the limits of practical cultivation. This was of little consequence during the period when sugar was all-important, but now that other crops form a large proportion of Surinam's agriculture, these limitations can no longer be ignored.

During the seventeenth and eighteenth centuries, however,

European wars and privateering raids were a greater source of worry than either topography or climate. The French, under Admiral Du Casse, attacked Surinam in 1689, but the colonists were able to drive off the invaders; in 1712, however, an attack by the French Admiral Jacques Cassard, with a fleet of thirty-eight vessels and approximately three thousand men, was more successful. Cassard sailed up the Surinam River and laid siege to Paramaribo and demanded its surrender. The governor demurred, but during the night part of the French fleet slipped past the city and pillaged the plantations farther up the river, in spite of the fact that the Dutch discovered the stratagem, and in the ensuing fight several of Cassard's vessels were damaged. The plantation owners, who feared for their lives as well as their property, brought pressure to bear upon the governor, who finally acceded to Cassard's demands and the colony was ransomed for 747,350 guilders, a sum far in excess of the gold and silver in the colony, the balance being paid in slaves and produce.

The financial loss to the colony, though staggering, was not so serious as the fact that during Cassard's attack many of the planters had fled, leaving their Negro slaves, who had remained only long enough to join the French in plundering the estates and then had escaped to the jungle. This constituted not only a serious loss of manpower in restoring the damage that had been done, but it also laid the foundation for subsequent slave insurrections, which in turn brought about abandonment of the outlying plantations, continual losses from raids, and a paralysis of effort from fear.

Surinam was now threatened from within as well as from without. Other Negroes had escaped a few at a time since the first days of slavery, but they had been unarmed; the escaped slaves now possessed weapons, and forays on isolated estates resulted in the seizure of more arms and ammunition.

The first general slave uprising occurred in 1730 on the Government plantation at Berg-en-Daal. From this time until the closing years of the century, the estate owners were never without fear for their lives, but the chief effect of the slave insurrections was to drive the wealthy planters into Paramaribo and to leave the plantations in charge of overseers, who treated the slaves with little humanity, with the result that there was a vicious circle of killings and reprisals on both sides.

Yet the eighteenth century was the most prosperous in Surinam's history. So great was the demand for its agricultural products in Europe that neither the difficulties of poldering, the losses from piracy and war, the effects of climate and disease on both planter and slave, the damage to crops by insects and plant diseases, nor the slave insurrections could entirely offset the profits.

7

The Slave Insurrections

SLAVERY, which had been introduced into the Caribbean at the beginning of the fifteenth century, received new impetus when the growing wealth of the plantation owners made it possible to import slaves not only as field workers, but as personal servants.

At first the bondman, whether Indian, Negro, or white, was a serf, rather than a slave. But the early settlers suffered few restraints, and it was not long before the power of life and death transformed serfdom into slavery, even as it had done centuries earlier in the Slavic countries, from which the name "slave" is derived. The early history of Española records that a certain number of Indians were attached to each parcel of land, and very often land was taken up more for the Indian laborers than for the land itself.

Slavery in the small islands of the West Indies was from the beginning less onerous than in Surinam. Conditions were better because of the tempering influence of the Roman Catholic Church, because escape was impossible and no stringent precautions were necessary to prevent it, because of the better climate and freedom from disease, and because field work on the island-plantations did not involve poldering. On the whole there was less difference between free men and slaves. This better treatment is acknowledged by the fact that many slaves in Curaçao were rented by their masters as sailors, yet they seldom made use of their opportunities to escape.

There were, of course, slave insurrections in the Caribbean islands, but it is probable that they were not all caused by ill treatment. The temperaments of slaves of different tribes differed considerably, and while some—like the Negroes and Paw Paws—were industrious, cheerful, and tractable, the Coromantees chafed under slavery and formed the focus of many uprisings. For this reason, it was forbidden to import them into the British colonies.

That Surinam could never have been developed without slavery is probably an overstatement, but it is no exaggeration to say that without it the development of all tropical regions in both North America and South America would have been greatly retarded and today might be no further advanced than some of the more remote and backward of the Pacific islands; for, unlike Europe, Asia, and Africa, the Americas were thinly populated by races that did not have the stamina to endure hard physical labor and who had little resistance to disease.

White races are incapable of plantation labor in the climate of Surinam, and if further proof of this statement is needed, it is only necessary to point to the Boeren, who, even as dairymen, are unable to hold their own in competition with the British Indians, in spite of the fact that they come from some of the sturdiest racial stock in Europe; and dairy farming scarcely can be compared to plantation labor. It was therefore necessary to discover a source of labor suitable to the climate, and the people of the teeming continent of Africa appeared to provide an ideal solution to the problem.

Slavery was not an invention of the European nations that exploited the Western Hemisphere. It was an established custom among the ancient Greeks and Romans, and for that matter was not unknown among the Negroes in their native Africa, where captives of war were often held as slaves; but the type of slavery that developed in the West Indies and the adjacent continental areas was different, in that the slaves were not prisoners of war. This new slavery was, instead, a deliberate effort by one race to exploit another.

The brutality practiced in the slave trade and on the plantations was at first no more than an extension of the greed that prompted this exploitation—the desire for riches at no matter what cost in human misery. It was an expression of the views of the time, just as the methods of the Inquisition in Europe—the ghetto, the press gang, and serfdom—were other expressions. It was more commonly the overseers, who were often soldiers of fortune inexperienced in agriculture, who were working to meet a quota, rather than plantation owners, who were responsible for the greatest excesses.

Sailors in the West Indies trade were treated with even less humanity than the slaves, for slaves in Surinam were valuable property. Sailors were required to load and unload the ships, carry the goods to the storehouses, row barges up-river to the plantations for cargoes of coffee and sugar, and even to row planters to their estates. All this was done to spare the more valuable Negro slaves, and if a ship's captain refused to allow his sailors to perform these services, which were no part of their calling, he was unable to get a cargo. Such was the power of the plantation owners.

To fully understand slavery in Surinam and the reasons which lay behind the slave insurrections, it is necessary to consult contemporary accounts, and it is fortunate that so excellent an observer as Captain Stedman should have written a book. Stedman, an Englishman, held a commission from the Dutch Government in the Scotts Brigade, which was sent to Surinam in 1773 to quell the slave insurrections. He spent five years in the colony and was married to a mulatto slave girl, the daughter of a wealthy plantation owner, who bore him a son. Consequently, he was well able to understand the problems of both planter and slave. His account of a Surinam planter, though written in 1783, nevertheless illustrates plantation life during the whole period of Surinam's development and deserves quoting at length:

A planter in Surinam, when he lives on his estate, (which is but seldom, as they mostly prefer the society of Paramaribo) gets out of his hammock with the rising sun, viz: about six in the morning, when he makes his appearance under the piazza of his house where his coffee is ready waiting for him. . . . There he is attended by half a dozen of the finest young slaves, both male and female, of the plantation, to serve him, and by his overseer, who having made his bow at several yards distance, with the most profound respect informs his Greatness what work was done the day before. . . .

The planter then metes out punishment to the slaves who are not allowed to say a word in their own defense. Next comes the "dressy Negro" (a black surgeon) who is dismissed with a hearty curse, for allowing any slaves to be sick, next makes her appearance a superannuated matron, with all the young negro children of the estate, over whom she is governess. . . .

His worship now saunters out in his morning dress, which consists of a pair of the finest Holland trousers, white silk stockings, and red or yellow morocco slippers; the neck of his shirt open, and nothing over it, a loose-flowing night-gown of the finest India chintz excepted. On his head is a cotton night-cap, as thin as a cobweb, and over that an enormous beaver hat, that protects his meagre visage from the sun, which is already the color of mahogany, while his whole carcass seldom weighs above eight or ten stone, being generally exhausted by the climate and dissipation. . . .

Having loitered about his estate, or sometimes ridden on horseback to his fields, to view his increasing stores, he returns about eight o'clock when, if he goes abroad, he dresses, but if not, remains just as he is. Should the first take place, having only exchanged his trousers for a pair of thin linen or silk breeches, he sits down, and holding out one foot after the other, like a horse going to be shod, a negro boy puts on his stockings and shoes, which he also buckles, while another dresses his hair, his wig, or shaves his chin, and a third is fanning him to keep off the mosquitoes. Having now shifted, he puts on a thin coat and waistcoat, all white; when, under an umbrella, carried by a black boy, he is conducted to his barge, which is in waiting for him, with five or six oars, well provided with fruit, wine, water, and tobacco. . . .

If he does not leave the estate, he breakfasts about ten at a table which is spread in the large hall, provided with a bacon ham, hung-beef, fowls, or pigeons broiled; plantains and sweet cassavas roasted; bread, butter, cheese, etc. with which he drinks strong beer, and a glass of Madeira, Rhenish, or Mozelle wine, while the cringing overseer sits at the farther end, keeping his proper distance, both being served by the most beautiful slaves that can be selected;— and this is called breaking the poor gentleman's fast.

After this he takes a book, plays at chess or billiards, entertains himself with music, etc. till the heat of the day forces him to return into his cotton hammock to enjoy his meridian nap . . . during which time he is fanned by a couple of his black attendants to keep him cool.

About three o'clock he awakes by natural instinct, when having washed and perfumed himself, he sits down to dinner, attended as at breakfast by his deputy-governor and sable pages, where nothing is wanting that the world can afford. . . . At six o'clock he is again waited on by his overseer, attended as in the morning by negro-drivers, and prisoners, when the flogging once more having continued for some time, and the necessary orders being given for the next day's work, the assembly is dismissed, and the evening spent with weak punch, sangaree, cards and tobacco.—His worship generally begins to yawn about ten or eleven o'clock when he withdraws and is undressed by his sooty pages. He then retires to rest, where he passes the night in the arms of one or other of his sable sultanas (for he always keeps a seraglio). . . .

Such absolute power indeed, cannot fail to be peculiarly delightful to a man, who, in all probability, was in his own country, Europe, a—nothing. . . . Exceptions, however, take place in every circumstance of life: and I have known many planters in Surinam as good men as I ever would desire to be acquainted with, which I have already mentioned.

As for the ladies, they indulge themselves just as much, by giving way to their unbounded passions, and especially to the most relentless barbarity. But while I can bear witness to the exalted virtues of a few women whose characters shine with treble lustre, I shall draw a veil over all the imperfections, too common to their sex in this climate. Before I drop this subject, however, I must attest, that hospitality is in no country practised with greater cordiality or with less ceremony.

It is not surprising that, under these conditions of dissipation and easy living on the part of the planter at the cost of abject misery for his slaves, there should have been insurrections.

Slave insurrections were not uncommon in the West Indies, but on the small islands they were easily put down by regular troops. In Surinam, however, the terrain greatly favored the Negroes. It was similar to their native Africa, and, as many of the Negroes escaped after a comparatively brief period of enslavement, they were able to revert to a pattern of life with which they were thoroughly familiar. They could walk naked and almost invisible through the jungle, while the Dutch troops scrambled after them, tearing their clothes and wetting their powder. The troops also suffered terribly from diseases to which the Negroes were practically immune, and the latter were able to exist on food grown in small provision grounds buried deep in the jungle, whereas the troops had a difficult problem of supply. It was, moreover, comparatively easy for the Negroes to avoid engaging the troops and for them to attack where they were least expected. This was the situation that confronted the colonists in 1730, when the first general uprising occurred at the Government plantation at Berg-en-daal.

The exigency was so great that the Government decided that drastic action must be taken, and eleven rebel Negroes who had been captured were executed in the most barbarous manner, as an example to the other rebels of what might be expected if they did not at once cease their depredations. But the consequence of this act was quite contrary to that intended and resulted in the escape of more slaves and further atrocities on both sides.

The Government, after an abortive campaign, was reduced to the humiliating expedient of seeking peace with the rebels, and a treaty was concluded in 1749 with Captain Adoe, the chief of the Saramacca rebels, in which the Government agreed to send the rebels a present of arms and ammunition the following year. The Governor, by a stroke of diplomacy, presented Captain Adoe with a cane with a silver pommel, on which were engraved the arms of Surinam. This was considered to be an acknowledgment of independence, but its acceptance was in fact an admission that independence was the Dutch Governor's to give, instead of its being a natural right. The distinction may have seemed small at the time, but the silver-headed cane is today an acknowledgment of Dutch rule, and the Dutch Governor holds the power of appointment of Bush Negro chiefs.

The treaty of peace with the Saramacca rebels was short-lived, for the following year the presents which were sent to Captain Adoe were intercepted by a rival chief by the name of Zam Zam, who was outraged by not having been consulted about the peace, and the entire party was massacred. The true facts were not known, and bad faith was suspected on both sides, with the result that the insurrection was renewed with even greater ferocity than before.

In 1757 another insurrection broke out at Tempaty Creek, and the colonists were no better able to cope with it than with the Saramacca insurrection, which was still in progress. The Government a second time was forced to sue for peace, and a treaty was successfully concluded in 1761 at the Ouca plantation. This treaty was signed by the rebel chief Araby and sixteen of his captains, and the white commissioners were obliged to take part in a ceremony in which a few drops of blood from each person were mixed in a calabash with clear spring water and a few particles of dry earth. The commissioners and the rebels alike then drank from the calabash, thereby sealing their oath.

A second peace was also concluded in the same year with the Saramacca rebels, but it again was broken when the chief Zam Zam captured the party that was delivering the gifts stipulated in the treaty, but this time he did not harm a single person. The colonists quickly learned what had happened, and a third and final treaty was concluded in 1762.

To quote Stedman again:

> The colony now seemed in a prosperous and flourishing state
> . . . and everything exhibited an aspect of peace and good order.
> The inhabitants believed their persons and effects in perfect se-
> curity, so that nothing was thought of but mirth and dissipation,
> which was soon extended to lavishness and profusion. Surinam re-
> sembled, indeed, a large and beautiful garden, stocked with every-
> thing that nature and art could produce, to make the life of man
> more comfortable to himself, and useful to society: all the luxuries,
> as well as all the necessaries of life, abounded; every sense was ap-
> parently intoxicated with enjoyment; and to use the figurative lan-
> guage of a sacred book, Surinam was a land that flowed with milk
> and honey.

The plantation owners quickly forgot the dangerous situation from which they had just escaped, and their new excesses laid the foundation for another insurrection which broke out on the Cottica River. This time the colonists resorted to the dangerous expedient of forming a regiment of slaves called Rangers, who were promised their freedom in return for fighting the rebels. The experiment was successful. Nevertheless, it was decided to ask the Prince of Orange to send a regular regiment from Europe, and this was granted.

The Scotts Brigade, of which Captain Stedman was an officer, landed at Paramaribo in February, 1773. It was composed of soldiers from many European countries, and was commanded by a Swiss officer, Colonel Fourgeoud. After five years of the most terrible hardships, the Brigade succeeded in destroying many of the rebel villages and provision grounds, and a number of the rebels who were facing starvation crossed the Marowijne River into French Guiana and placed themselves under the protection of the French Government.

The manumitted Rangers and the rebels became deadly enemies, and no mercy was shown on either side, but few of the European soldiers were actually killed in battle. Due to hardship, disease, and climatic conditions, however, less than a hundred of the original twelve hundred men survived and probably not more than one in five of these was in good health when he returned to Europe.

All organized resistance was destroyed by this campaign and the last of the slave insurrections came to a gradual end. This time there was no treaty, only an armed truce. Both the rebels and the colonists had had enough of fighting. The planters could now return to the cultivation of their estates, but only a few years later this success was offset by the capture of Surinam by the English and its isolation from the markets of Europe.

In the end, the victory lay neither with the rebels nor with the planters, but with an increasing sensibility in the civilized world of the rights of man. It was a victory of humanity over greed, and it is a mark of our progress that slavery today should seem barbarous and unnecessarily cruel. The final battle has not been won. There are still traces of resentment in the population which are deep-rooted in the past and will not be eradicated until men of all races and colors and creeds can learn to work together for a common cause without prejudice or fear. But Surinam has already made great progress along that path.

Decline in the Caribbean

8

Forty Years of War

THE American colonies from the beginning of their history had been subject to the vagaries of European politics, and they had variously been exploited by the Dutch, British, and French West India companies. European rule often had been resented by the colonists, many of whom had come to the New World to be free of just such domination, and this resentment was expressed openly in the refusal to comply with the arbitrary laws promulgated by the home governments. But on May 19, 1755, this spark was fanned into open flame, and with the beginning of the American Revolution, liberal ideas, long suppressed, were released.

France found in the Revolution an opportunity to carry on her war with the English, and pressure was brought to bear on the Dutch to allow the use of Netherlands ports to ship goods and arms to the revolutionists.

The sympathy of a large majority of the Dutch people was on the side of the revolutionists, whose struggle must have reminded them of their own long fight for freedom with Spain. But the Dutch were in no position to defy British naval strength. Dutch power had declined since the reign of William and Mary, when Dutch interests first had been subordinated to those of Britain, and the Government long had been in the hands of a few self-seeking individuals who had been willing to subordinate the good of the country to their own ends.

The maritime provinces, foreseeing a war with England, had been anxious to increase the size of the navy, but the inland provinces had been unwilling to contribute their share. The representatives of the various provinces were unable to come to any agreement, with the result that nothing was done. Several years later, when it was finally decided to rebuild the fleet, it was too late and the Dutch were able to muster only twenty ships against more than three hundred of Britain.

Curaçao and St. Eustatius both profited greatly by the American Revolution, but it was St. Eustatius that played the major role in supplying arms and ammunition to North America. This small island became the meeting place of French and American agents, and even the British merchants from the surrounding islands continued to trade with North America, for they were unwilling to forego the profits offered in business and, furthermore, many felt more sympathy for the colonists than for the government in England. This contraband trade became so remunerative that, even if two out of three ships were lost to the British cruisers, there was still a profit. In 1778 and 1779, 3,000 ships anchored in the St. Eustatius roadstead. It is no wonder that the island came to be known as "The Golden Rock."

Janet Schaw, who landed on the island on January 19, 1775, described the island in these words:

In a few hours after we left St. Kitts, we landed on St. Eustatia, a free port, which belonged to the Dutch; a place of vast traffick from every quarter of the globe. The ships of various nations which rode before it were very fine, but the Island itself the only ugly one I have seen. Nor do I think that I would stay on it for any bribe. It is however an instance of Dutch industry little inferior to their dykes; as the one half of the town is gained off the Sea, which is fenced out by

Barracadoes, and the other dug out of an immense mountain of sand and rock; which rises to a great height behind the houses, and will one day bury them under it. On the top of this hill I saw some decent-looking houses, but was not able to mount it, to look at them nearer. I understand however that the whole riches of the Island consist in its merchandize, and that they are obliged to the neighbouring Islands for subsistence; while they in return furnish them with contraband commodities of all kinds. The town consists of one street a mile long, but very narrow and most disagreeable, as every one smokes tobacco, and the whiffs are constantly blown in your face.

But never did I meet with such variety. . . . From one end of the town of Eustatia to the other is a continued mart, where goods of the most different uses and qualities are displayed before the shop-doors.

Edmund Burke in his *Account of the European Settlements in America* further states that:

The trade of this island, even in times of peace, is reputed to be worth to the Dutch, no less than 500,000 £ sterling annually, but in time of war the profit is far greater, for then it is in a manner the common emporium of the West-Indies; it affords a great retreat to the ships of all nations, and at the same time refuses to none of them arms and ammunition to annoy one another.

The English could not afford to ignore the role that St. Eustatius was playing, and time after time Sir Joseph Yorke, the English Ambassador to the Netherlands, protested to the States General; but he received scant satisfaction. French and American agents at the same time were pleading their cause in Holland and, most important, the Dutch had no intention of relinquishing this profitable trade if they could avoid such a course.

The States General resented the insolence of the British demands, and Sir Joseph Yorke heightened this resentment by an arrogance of manner that could not fail to be distasteful to a people jealous of their independence.

The States General adopted a policy of evasion, countering all British demands with promises to consider them, yet seldom reaching decisions. In this they were more clever than the British, who presented a hundred petty complaints which tended to obscure the real issue and allowed the States General to evade it. They disclaimed each fresh violation of neutrality that was brought to their attention as the act of a private citizen over which they had no control; and time after time orders were issued that all trade in contraband was to cease, but these orders were never enforced.

A few efforts were made to appease the British, and van Heyliger, the Governor of St. Eustatius, actually was replaced by Johannes de Graaff, but with results quite contrary to those desired by the British.

At this time two events further widened the breach between the two countries. The British claimed that one of their merchantmen was taken as a prize by an American privateer under the very guns of Fort Oranje, but the Dutch insisted that this had happened out of range of the fort and that they certainly could not have prevented it. But there was no attempt to excuse the second incident. On November 16, 1776, Fort Oranje was ordered by de Graaff to fire a salute to the American brig, *Andrew Doria,* which sailed into the roadstead flying the flag of thirteen red and white stripes of the American colonies.

The incident was reported to the British governor of the neighboring island of St. Kitts, who had no sooner heard of it than he sent a protest to de Graaff at what he considered a direct insult to Britain—the virtual recognition of a revolutionary government. The Dutch Governor's reply was not one of appeasement, for he broke off the correspondence with the blunt statement that he was responsible to no one but the States General and was not obligated to give an account of his actions to anyone else.

This affair eventually reached the courts of Europe, and after many months, due to the delays of communication by sailing ship, as well as to the obstructive policy of the States General, de Graaff was recalled to Holland to explain his actions. But there is every evidence that this was a mere formality and a sop to British pride, for he was later allowed to return to the island with scarcely a reprimand.

A further incident—the appearance of the *Bon Homme Richard,* commanded by John Paul Jones and flying the American flag, in the harbor of Amsterdam with two British ships that he had taken as prizes in the North Sea—brought the British accusation that the Dutch, contrary to international law, were harboring pirates. But the members of the States General were too long committed to their policy of evasion to change their tactics. They made a few attempts to prove that Jones was sailing under a commission from France, and a French commission was even obtained to bear out this story; but Jones refused to change his colors. He was, nevertheless, allowed to remain for three months in Amsterdam, and all demands to turn the ships over to the British were refused.

Four years of fruitless discussion finally convinced the British that nothing was to be gained by diplomacy, and on December 20, 1780, war was declared on the Netherlands. Orders were sent by a fast ship to Admiral Rodney, who was already cruising in the Caribbean, to attack St. Eustatius, and he immediately embarked troops at St. Lucia and appeared in the roadstead of St. Eustatius on February 3, 1781. The inhabitants of the island, unaware that they were at war with England, were unprepared for an attack, and when Rodney demanded the surrender of the island with all its stores, Governor de

Graaff considered it useless to resist. One hundred and fifty vessels which were in the roadstead fell to the British, and twenty-six merchant ships, which had sailed in convoy the previous day, were captured by one of Rodney's captains and added to the booty. Rodney's dishonorable expedient of ordering the Dutch flag to remain flying over Fort Oranje resulted in many more vessels falling into British hands; one report mentions the number as two hundred and fifty, and Rodney in a letter says that fifty American vessels alone were captured in the first two months of the British occupation.

Rodney was amazed at the wealth of St. Eustatius. When he saw that the long line of stone warehouses were so full that the less perishable goods had to be left on the beach, he declared that, had it not been for this island, the American Revolution could not have lived, and it is estimated that half of the munitions for the Continental Army were transshipped at St. Eustatius.

Rodney set himself the task of completely destroying the lower town and all of the harbor installations. The breakwater and the cofferdam were dismantled, and the sea was allowed to finish the work of destruction.

Even the goods of the British residents were confiscated, and all foreigners were ordered to leave the island. Thirty-four fully-laden ships were dispatched to England under escort and other booty was sent to the nearby British colonies. The remainder was sold at a great auction that netted the present-day equivalent of fifteen million dollars.

Though the British achieved their main objective, which was the complete destruction of St. Eustatius as a base of supplies for the revolutionists, they received little further profit from the enterprise, for none of the thirty-four ships reached England, twenty-two being captured by a French fleet and the remaining twelve by French and American privateers. Rodney's long delay at St. Eustatius also allowed the various units of the French fleet to re-form and sail for Yorktown, with serious consequences to the British cause in North America. Furthermore, many of the goods that were sold at auction eventually found their way to North America from the neighboring islands, and the charge was brought that, whereas Rodney had accused the merchants of St. Eustatius with supplying the revolutionists, he had done the same thing himself—only at cheaper rates. This affair later was debated at length in Parliament.

A final blow to the British in St. Eustatius was the capture of the island by the French on November 26, when 250,000 pounds sterling, which had been earmarked for the payment of British troops in North America, fell into French hands.

The attack on St. Eustatius served warning on the other Dutch colonies, and Surinam and Curaçao were able to prepare for their successful defense; but Berbice, Demerara, and Essequebo, as well as the islands of Saba and St. Martin, fell into British hands.

Peace finally was concluded between Great Britain and the Netherlands on May 20, 1784, but the Dutch West India Company, which for years had been in a precarious financial position, had suffered disastrous losses, due to the neglect of the sugar plantations in the Guiana colonies and to the seizure of its ships during the war. The company was liquidated when its charter expired in 1791, and its colonies came under the jurisdiction of the States General.

The French Revolution, meanwhile, had set in motion events which were to change the face of Europe and which were to be reflected in the West Indies. Slaves in the French colonies were given their independence, only to have it snatched from them in a few short months. The result was bloodshed. The island of Española was thrown into a turmoil of revolution and counter-revolution, and in Haiti the Negroes revolted and massacred the entire white population. Santo Domingo revolted, was subdued, and revolted again, only to be captured by the Haitians. Ideas of "liberty, equality, fraternity" struck a responsive chord in all the islands of the Caribbean and the days of slavery were numbered.

Life in the Netherlands, because of oppression, had become intolerable to many free-thinking Dutchmen and they had fled to France, where they conspired against the hereditary stadtholder, the Prince of Orange. A French army invaded the Netherlands in 1795 after the stadtholder had fled to England, and the Batavian Republic was proclaimed. But there was little realization in the Netherlands at this time that freedom had been purchased by a foreign power. It was never believed that the French, who had so recently fought for their own freedom, would plan the conquest of another country. Yet in France thoughts had already turned from revolution to the militant propagation of their recently acquired concepts. They recognized the Batavian Republic as an independent state, but they demanded that 25,000 French troops be garrisoned in the Netherlands at the expense of the Dutch and that a loan of 100,000 guilders be made to France, together with the outright gift of a similar sum. Furthermore, they laid claim to territory in the southern Netherlands. An agreement finally was reached between the French Government and the Batavian Republic on May 16, 1795, and as a result the long-standing treaty between the Netherlands and Great Britain was broken and the British fleet blockaded the Dutch coast.

The situation was complicated further when the exiled Prince of Orange sent letters with the commanders of the British warships ordering the Dutch colonies to accept British protection. At the same time, the Batavian Republic laid claim to jurisdiction over the colonies, and a hopelessly confused situation resulted. Public opinion in Surinam forced the Governor to declare allegiance to the Republic, but in 1799 the colony was compelled to surrender to a superior British force under Lord Seymour. On the other hand, many people in Curaçao refused to take orders from the director sent out by the Batavian Republic, but when the French in Guadeloupe offered to support the new director, their help was refused. Notwithstanding this refusal, the French occupied the island in 1800 to prevent its falling into English hands.

St. Eustatius, which had suffered so severely at the hands of Rodney in 1780, was captured by the French in 1795 and the population was not only forced to pay for the garrisoning of the French troops, but to contribute a monthly indemnity of 8,000 Spanish florins as well. The latter soon proved to be an impossibility, for the population was by this time totally impoverished, and many thousands of people left the island, in spite of laws enacted to prevent their departure. In 1801 the French withdrew their troops, and in the same year the British occupied the island and also captured Curaçao.

The Treaty of Amiens on March 27, 1802, brought about the restoration of all the Dutch possessions, but 1803 saw the beginning of the Napoleonic wars. One by one the Dutch colonies again capitulated to stronger British forces: Surinam surrendered in 1804; Curaçao, Aruba, and Bonaire on January 1, 1807; and St. Eustatius on February 21, 1810.

The pretense of Dutch autonomy was abandoned in 1806 when the Batavian Republic was dissolved at the demand of Napoleon. Louis Bonaparte was then constituted monarch of the new Kingdom of Holland. Louis accepted the throne only under the belief that it was the wish of the Dutch people, and he did his best to give Holland a just government, but by doing so he was forced to go counter to the wishes of Napoleon; and on July 1, 1810, realizing the futility of his position, he abdicated the throne. Nine days later Napoleon annexed Holland to the French Empire.

Napoleon's bloody campaigns finally came to an end on April 7, 1814, and he was forced to abdicate and was sent into exile. Though he returned the following year for "The Hundred Days," the Peace of Paris and the London Convention of 1814 settled the fate of the colonies. Surinam and the Dutch West Indies islands were returned to the Netherlands. Berbice, Demerara, and Essequebo, however, were ceded to Great Britain, and the Netherlands received compensation equal to six million pounds sterling. These treaties brought to an end thirty years of almost continuous warfare and established the political geography of the West Indian islands in its present form.

9

One Hundred Years of Neglect:
1816-1915

THE end of the Napoleonic wars found the fortunes of the Dutch colonies in the Caribbean at a low ebb. For forty years the West Indies had been isolated from its markets in Europe, and the shifting of administration from the West India Company to the States General to the Batavian Republic to the various governments of occupation had proved to be an extremely unsettling factor.

Curaçao was in a state bordering on starvation, with its commerce destroyed and its plantations ruined, and the trade of St. Eustatius had been transferred to the Danish island of St. Thomas following Rodney's depredations and the English and French occupations, and it was not recovered due to the fact that the island lacked the basic requirements of an entrepôt and its importance had been brought about only through sheer persistence on the part of the Dutch merchants.

The condition of Surinam was no better, and to make matters worse, Paramaribo experienced two disastrous fires in 1821 and 1832 which destroyed half of the city. The immense fortunes based on the cultivation of sugar had declined due to the war and many of the plantations had been neglected and had reverted to jungle. Furthermore, a beet-sugar industry had been established in Europe during the period when cane had been cut off, and, as it had been encouraged by bounties in many

105

countries, it now provided formidable competition to the sugar of the Surinam estates.

The one stabilizing influence in the Caribbean in the midst of so many uncertainties was the promulgation of the Monroe Doctrine by the United States in 1823.

The American and French Revolutions had brought to an end an era of privilege and had turned the thoughts of men to liberty and equality for all people. Governments in Europe began to debate the ethics of slavery and on January 1, 1808, the British prohibited the further importation of slaves into their colonies and the other colonies under their control. No slaves, therefore, were imported into Surinam between that date and 1815, when the trade was resumed. The last cargo of slaves was brought from Africa in 1819 and traffic with North America ceased in 1821.

In the three preceding centuries more than ten million slaves had been brought to the Americas alive, and it is estimated that during this period another forty million Negroes were killed in slave raids or died in the African slave factories or on the slave ships. This constituted an enormous loss to the African continent and substantially retarded its development.

There was great unrest among the slaves throughout the entire Caribbean area following the cessation of the slave trade, for it now seemed certain that emancipation would take place in the near future, and the imaginations of the slaves were fired by the prospect of freedom.

The emancipation of 750,000 slaves in the British colonies in 1834 caused further unrest in the Dutch and French possessions. The French followed the British example in 1848, and this brought about even more severe repercussions in the Dutch islands. There was a slave insurrection in St. Eustatius, and in St. Martin the planters, fearing a similar occurrence and realizing that it would be a simple matter for the slaves to escape into French territory, petitioned the Government to emancipate the slaves on the island immediately, feeling that it was better to receive an indemnity rather than to risk losing the slaves without compensation. This petition, however, was denied on the ground that it would be impossible to free the slaves in one part of Dutch territory without doing so in the other parts.

The plantation owners found themselves in the difficult position of being forced on their own account to grant their slaves freedom in all but name, and for many years they traded with them as though they were free men.

The delay of the States General in reaching a decision on emancipation also proved costly in Surinam, where many of the plantations which had been heavily mortgaged were abandoned, with a resulting loss to businessmen in the Netherlands.

Finally, after interminable discussion, emancipation of the slaves in the Dutch colonies took place on July 1, 1863. Forty-five thousand two hundred and seventy-five slaves were set free with the proviso that those between the ages of fifteen and sixty should continue to work for a wage for a period of ten years.

An indemnity of three hundred guilders was paid for each slave in Surinam, whereas in the islands this figure was reduced to two hundred guilders, with the exception of St. Martin where compensation was set at thirty guilders, on the ground that the slaves there had enjoyed their freedom for some time and were of less value to the plantation owners. This was an affront to the planters who had previously pled for emancipation, and although the indemnity was increased to one hundred guilders the following year, many of the planters had become so disgusted with the treatment that they had received that they left the island, taking with them the capital which could have saved it from the total economic collapse which ensued.

In Saba, where the white proprietors had worked side by side with their slaves in the fields and where the slaves had often been treated as members of the families, emancipation caused very little dislocation of the economic system. Aruba and Bonaire also were little affected, for Aruba was largely undeveloped and the entire island of Bonaire was a single Government plantation until 1867, when the land at either end of the island was sold in large tracts, though the central district was retained by the Government and is still rented out to small farmers.

In Surinam, where labor had always been scarce, and where agriculture rather than trade had been paramount, the condition became impossible, for the population plainly was insufficient to develop the country except under a slave economy. A comparison of the population of Surinam with that of several other countries reveals its deficiency even today for, whereas Surinam has a density of only 3.3 persons to the square mile, including Bush Negroes and Amerindians, the United States as a whole averages 45, New York State 275, the Netherlands 693, and Java 822 persons to the square mile, respectively; and it has only been since 1900 that Surinam's population has substantially exceeded one person to the square mile. It is not an exaggeration to say that, if the problem of a sufficient and a dependable labor supply were solved, it would bring with it the answer to many of Surinam's agricultural problems.

The average number of slaves brought to Surinam annually between the years 1650 and 1826 was between 1,500 and 2,000 —a total of perhaps a quarter of a million. Yet today the Negroes and mulattoes total only 70,415. There are several reasons for this: (1) there was a preponderance of males over females; (2) the Negro birth rate was low under the severe conditions imposed by slavery; (3) infant mortality, always high among Negroes, due to the carelessness of the Negro mothers, was higher under slavery in spite of all the planters could do to protect the Negro children, which they considered to be their property; (4) contrary to general opinion, the death rate from disease was high, and it is likely that part of the Negroes' reputation for laziness was due to disease, rather than to a lack of desire to work. Recent statistics show that the Negro death rate from tuberculosis, cancer, pneumonia, and heart disease is higher than for either the British Indians or the Javanese.

The Negroes, since emancipation, have suffered from the feeling that all field work is degrading. In a few cases Negroes have settled on old estates, sometimes occupying the houses of their former masters, but even in their native Africa Negroes are poor agriculturists, and most of these estates are to be found in a state of dilapidation reminiscent of many of our abandoned plantations in the South.

Many Negroes and mulattoes find employment in the gold placers, become boatmen on the lower rivers, or work in the bauxite plants and on the railroads, where they are competent mechanics. Many hold positions in the Government and teach in the schools. Others become clerks in the stores, chauffeurs and servants in Paramaribo, sailors on the river boats or soldiers in the local army. A large percentage prefers to live in Paramaribo—in spite of the fact that there is often insufficient employment—refusing to be resettled in rural areas even when they are impoverished.

The Negro has lost touch with his own culture and has patterned his conduct and his ideals after those of the white man; but in spite of notions of independence, many Negroes have the idea that they owe nothing to society and that the best way of showing their complete independence is by idleness. They wish to enjoy the white man's privileges without accepting his responsibilities, and they expect the Government to support them, to care for their children, to provide them with food and medicine, and to house them, as the plantation owners did in the days of slavery. In short, the consequences of slavery in Surinam have been very little different than in other countries. The Negro was made dependent and scarcely has relearned the fundamentals of freedom. He was not naturally lazy, but he became lazy when he had nothing personal to gain from his work. If something is not done to overcome these basic misconceptions of his place in society, he will become the economic slave of other races who are more willing to accept their responsibilities and who are more ambitious.

Immigration is the only possible solution if Surinam is to regain its importance as an agricultural colony; consequently, various attempts have been made to find suitable colonists. The first to come to Surinam following the cessation of the slave trade were Dutch farmers, though it is inconceivable how experienced Government officials could have permitted them to immigrate in the light of past experience—the disastrous white colonization of French Guiana and the fact that the Dutch planters in Surinam, who did no manual work at all, found the climate all but insupportable.

The plan for colonization by Dutch farmers was conceived by three clergymen, who submitted it to King William III and who subsequently were put in charge of the immigrants; but their judgment and their ability to organize the plan were lacking.

The first group of farmers, or Hollandsche Boeren, arrived in 1845 and settled on the deserted plantation of Voorburg and at Groningen. They found that very inadequate provisions had been made for them. There were no proper accommodations, and no arable land had been prepared.

It is quite impossible for a white man, even of the sturdiest peasant stock, to do the heavy work of poldering and field labor in tropical lowlands such as those of Surinam, though he is fresh from Europe; and a protracted stay, rather than acclimatizing the European, tends to reduce his resistance. It is not surprising then that, of these 384 ill-fed and ill-housed settlers, 189 contracted typhus and died within a few months. Fifty-six returned to the Netherlands, others moved to the upper Surinam River, and a third group settled in the neighborhood of Paramaribo and formed the nucleus of the existing colony.

The Hollandsche Boeren today number 490, "persons with one parent and one grandparent of Surinam blood" excepted, but there are few families—probably not more than half a dozen —that can claim to have no mixed blood. The Boeren have been forced to intermarry to retain their racial identity at all, and many people are of the opinion that this has affected them physically and intellectually. I found them, however, surprisingly sturdy, animated, and mentally alert for white people with a background of nearly one hundred years in the worst type of tropical climate.

The greatest number of Boeren have become small dairy farmers and they derive an inadequate income from selling milk, chickens, eggs, and vegetables in Paramaribo. But competition from the British Indians has become increasingly strong in recent years and the lot of the Boeren proportionately difficult. As A. Grenfell Price in *White Settlers in the Tropics* points out: if a white race survives all the other hazards of the tropics, it is usually only to give way before a colored people who are willing to accept a lower standard of living.

Between 1852 and 1872, 480 Madeirans and 2,502 Chinese immigrated to Surinam, but the former were able to acclimatize themselves little better than the Boeren, and many of the Chinese left Surinam at the end of their indentures. Subsequent Chinese immigrants, though valuable colonists, did not solve the problems of plantation labor, for unlike the Chinese in Curaçao, they have abandoned agriculture to become shop-keepers.

Large-scale immigration has been confined to British Indians and to Indonesians, the latter primarily Javanese.

British Indians had been brought to British Guiana and to Trinidad as contract laborers since 1838, and experience had proved that they were adaptable and that they did not demand a very high standard of living. British Indian immigration, therefore, appeared to be an ideal solution to Surinam's labor problem.

An agreement was reached between the Netherlands and Britain on September 8, 1870, but the first British Indians did not arrive in Surinam until 1873.

The terms of their contract bound them to work for five years for a minimum wage of sixty cents a day for men and forty cents a day for women; free housing and a working day of seven hours were also provided for. At the end of their indenture they were guaranteed a free passage home.

Anti-slavery proponents were quick to seize on contract labor as another "cause" and to label it as a new slavery, in spite of the fact that all coolies were subject to the strictest supervision by an Agent General and that they in reality were far freer than they had ever been in India, because of the removal of caste restrictions.

Some trouble was experienced at first because the barriers of language made it necessary to employ overseers accustomed to handling coolie labor in the East. These overseers were accused of unnecessary harshness, but they countered this accusation with the reply that they treated the coolies no differently than in India and that, in any case, it was the only way to get them to work. As a result of this controversy, even stricter regulations were put into effect and immigration was continued after a short interruption.

The first British Indian coolies had been conscripted from the dregs of Calcutta and had no previous knowledge of agriculture. They were, therefore, far from satisfactory as plantation laborers and, though later immigrants were of a better class, the emphasis appears to have been on quantity, rather than on quality.

People of the East have a very strong attachment to their own communities and, as they have long been accustomed to the effects of overpopulation and scarcity, it is not easy to convince them of the advantages of pioneering in a new country. They have ties of tradition, family, and religion, and they cannot appreciate the opportunities and the freedom that are offered to them. Consequently, it is only the most oppressed classes—the failures, the misfits, and the radicals—that will consent to emigrate.

A very few Javanese came to Surinam as free settlers between the years 1853 and 1893, but it was only in 1894 that an enlistment office was opened in Java. The same difficulty of securing a good class of immigrant, however, was experienced with the Javanese as had heretofore been the case with the British Indians.

Between 1873 and 1916, when emigration from British India was stopped, a total of 34,024 British Indians came to Surinam and of these 11,650 were repatriated, whereas only 7,228 of the 32,020 Indonesians who came to Surinam as contract laborers between 1874 and 1931 returned to Java.

Both the British Indians and the Javanese have a long background of civilization, yet they are very different. The British Indians are, as a rule, aggressive, self-interested, and politically ambitious. They were found to be troublesome on many of the plantations and few of them were content to remain as plantation laborers after their contracts expired. In their new environment they have rid themselves of the fetters of caste, many have become small agricultural free-holders, and they are now to be found in all of the professions and as businessmen and politicians. There are three British Indians in the Legislative Council.

The British Indians are divided between Hindus and Mohammedans in a ratio of about three to one. There is none of the religious fanaticism of India, and they appear to have resolved their religious animosities. But though they have made this concession to their new environment, they have otherwise changed little. Surinam has been notably successful in its role as the melting pot of races, but in spite of all propaganda to the contrary, the British Indians have not been assimilated. They remain British Indians, with a distinct racial consciousness.

The Javanese ideology is quite different. Though they are universally Mohammedans, theirs is not the militant Mohammedanism of the Mediterranean countries, but a Mohammedanism that reflects the meekness of their earlier Hindu background. For this reason they get along well with the other races in Surinam.

Whereas the energy of the British Indians is directed toward self-aggrandizement or, at best, family interests, the Javanese think in the broader terms of the *desa,* the village community.

The birth rate of the Javanese is not as high as that of the British Indians, and their death rate is also lower. They are less susceptible to disease than other races in Surinam. Though the British Indian is stronger and a faster worker, the Javanese is more dependable. He is an experienced agriculturist and exposure to Western culture has not changed him. He still is willing to remain an agriculturist.

At the expiration of their contracts, immigrants receive 100 guilders and a plot of land from the Government, but in recent

British Indian Actor.

Carib Indian Girl in Dance Costume.

Old Woman from Coronie.

Sluice Gates at Coronie.

Granman with his Wife and Captains.

Government Building at Paramaribo.

Old Jewish Cemetery at Curaçao.

The Fort at Kralendijk, Bonaire.

Curaçao Plantation.

Water Cart, Willemstad.

St. Nicolaas—Boom Town.

Husking Coconuts, Coronie.

Typical House, St. Martin.

St. Eustatius Coast Line.

Boat Day at Kralendijk.

Bush Negro Corials on the Pikien Rio.

"Dansi-Dansi" at Curaçao.

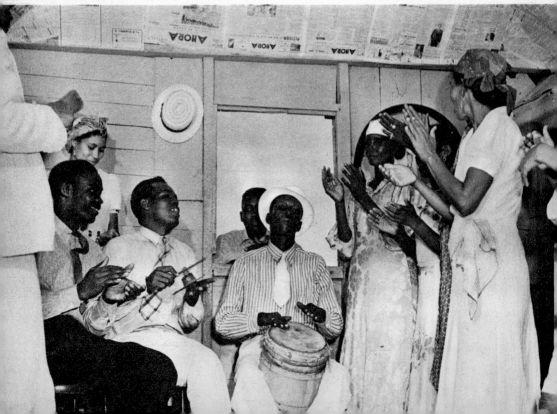

Sloop "Atlantic."

Saba Fisherman.

Curaçao Woodcutter.

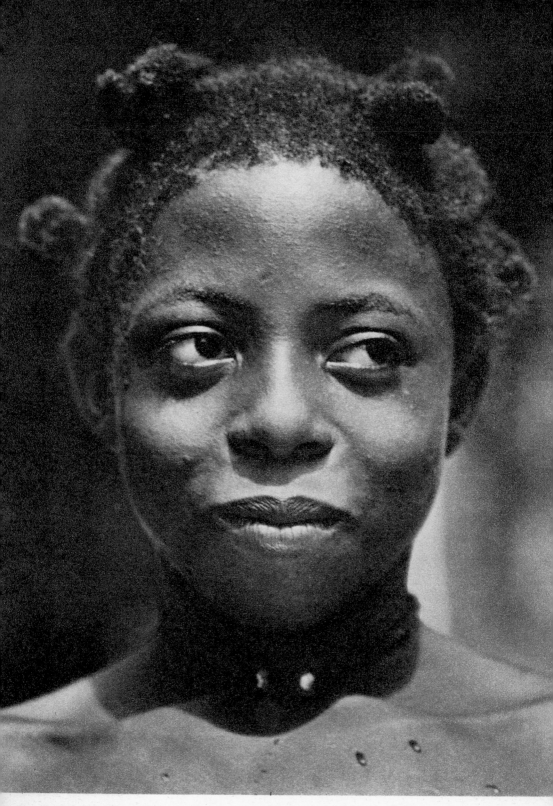

Bush Negro Boy.

years, many workers have preferred to remain on the plantations rather than to chance the uncertainties of independent ownership.

It is possible that the *desa* will be the solution to Surinam's agricultural problems, for it is a group welded together by common interests. The bond may not be as strong as it was in Java, but the *desa* is bound by racial inheritance and a common respect for *adat,* the traditional religious and secular law of the Javanese people. The *desas* may be able to approximate the efficiency of the large estates for they will have the added incentive of communal ownership and self-interest.

Immigration of contract laborers from Java was stopped in 1931, but several shiploads of free immigrants have come to Surinam since that time.

The population of Java is increasing by 750,000 annually, and it is to be hoped that after the war some arrangement can be made to continue Javanese emigration to Surinam. There are a number of reasons, however, why this may not be possible: (1) Prior to the war, Javanese were being used to develop the thinly populated islands of the East Indies, and although only a small proportion of the surplus population was resettled in this way, plans were already in effect to develop the outer islands on a much larger scale. (2) There is a difference of opinion as to whether the Javanese immigrants are satisfied with their life in Surinam and whether they will be willing to emigrate to the Western Hemisphere, unless they are forced to do so by far greater economic pressures than have yet been brought to bear upon them. Both Javanese and British Indian contract laborers have in the past come from the coolie class and have brought with them little culture. This in one sense is an advantage, for it reduces the differences between the various races rather than emphasizes them, for the lower levels of any culture tend to be more alike and therefore to fuse more easily. On the other hand, the transference of culture would have the effect of making the immigrant feel more at home in his new environment. (3) The other nations of the Western Hemisphere may object to a large migration of oriental labor as tending to lower the standards of living or to compete unfairly with those nations having a higher living standard. In this connection, however, it should be pointed out that the present wage scale of Surinam is much higher than that of Brazil.

The difficulties that confronted the West Indian colonies in the nineteenth century appeared even greater when contrasted with the increasingly bright prospects of Java. The East Indies' tremendous reserves of natural resources and almost limitless supply of cheap labor with which to exploit them were made more accessible to Europe by the replacement of the sailing ship by the steamship, and by the opening of the Suez Canal in 1869, the traveling time between Java and Europe was again greatly reduced. This condition inevitably resulted in a lessening of interest in the West Indies colonies by the Netherlands Government, a condition that was duplicated in the West Indies colonies of the other European powers.

The discovery of gold on Aruba in 1825 aroused some interest in this hitherto undeveloped island. For the first few years the mines were worked by the Government, but when they failed to produce a sufficient amount of gold to make the venture profitable, concessions were granted to private companies. The report of one of these companies, the Aruba Gold Mining Company, Ltd., for 1872 is interesting, both for its description of the island and because of its optimistic tone. At that time there were no roads on Aruba and all goods were transported by donkey, for there were no wheeled vehicles on the island. The native laborers in the mines received seventy-five cents for a day's work of nine hours, a price fixed by the Government; and the report calls these people "industrious, quiet, peaceable, obedient, and very easy to control."

One of the difficulties of mining was the lack of water. "There is only one natural spring on the island which is always flowing. Drinking water is taken from wells sunk in solid rock far enough from the sea to prevent its being brakish. Almost everywhere on the island water is found by sinking wells to some depth, usually only a few feet below sea level, but most of the water used on the island is rainwater." In spite of this, the report concludes, "the accessibility of the island by water, the fact that there will be little or no land carriage for the machinery, fuel and other supplies, as well as ore, bullion, etc., the honest and peaceable character of the inhabitants and their complete control by the Government officials, the low price and quality of the native labor, the great benefit to be derived from the use of wind as motive power, the width and richness of the principal veins, and the facility with which the ores can be mined—all combine to make the Aruba Island Gold Mining Company one of the most promising enterprises for mining gold."

In spite of this optimistic report, the Company failed and by the beginning of the twentieth century gold mines had been abandoned to the local inhabitants, who panned the gold in a crude fashion and managed to make a precarious living. Free gold, however, became increasingly more difficult to find, and by 1911 the census indicates that the island had returned to agriculture.

Gold was discovered in Surinam in 1875, and in 1905-1911 a railroad was built for the purpose of opening up the gold fields. But neither the railroad nor gold mining has ever been profitable. Attempts to mine gold on a large scale in Surinam have all failed, due to the difficulties of transport, the climate, and the fact that none of the placers is particularly rich.

At the present time most gold is washed on a small scale by "pork knockers," individual operators, generally Negroes, some of whom find this work profitable because they are able to operate with virtually no overhead, but even they cannot always make a living from washing gold. About a thousand pounds of gold is mined annually, and all of it is now bought by the Surinam Bank.

The excellent harbor at Willemstad had been one of the chief reasons for the original Dutch occupation of the island, and the first thought of the Dutch when they regained control of Curaçao in 1816 was to revive it as a world shipping center. Toward this end Willemstad had been made a free port in 1828, and a certain amount of success was attained in reestablishing its position as a transshipment port for the northern coast of Venezuela.

In 1881 the Royal Dutch West India Mail—Koninklijke West-Indische Maildienst—was organized in Amsterdam, and three years later started operating a regular steamship service between Holland, Curaçao, and Paramaribo. In 1888 the service was extended to New York via Haiti.

The Royal Dutch West India Mail was absorbed in 1912 by the Royal Netherlands Steamship Company—Koninklijke Nederlandsche Stoomboot Maatschappij N.V.—and the expansion of services progressed steadily, in spite of several depressions. A number of other steamship lines also made Curaçao a regular port of call.

The Government looked forward to the opening of the Panama Canal as the beginning of a new epoch, and in anticipation coral reefs at the entrance to the harbor were blasted and mud was dredged out, so that ships up to 35,000 tons could enter the Schottegat. Coal bunkering facilities were also installed, but any hopes that had been held that Curaçao would regain its dominating position in the southern Caribbean area were largely unrealized. Modern ships no longer required frequent stops for refueling, and the fact that Colon, with its more central location, had also been made a bunkering port destroyed the value of Curaçao for this purpose.

Agriculture on Curaçao was limited to the cultivation of aloes, divi-divi pods for tanning, and a small number of oranges which were used in the manufacture of the well-known Curaçao liqueur. The weaving of straw hats from palmetto imported from Venezuela was the most important home industry. Phosphate had been discovered at Newport in 1875, but the quarry was not developed on a large scale until after the war. It was also mined for several years on Aruba and Little Curaçao but was unprofitable, and work was discontinued. Agriculture in Aruba was even less productive than in Curaçao and barely supported the native population, and Bonaire and the Windward Islands were in a similar condition.

The future of Curaçao certainly did not seem very bright at this time, and Herdman F. Cleland in his article *Curaçao, A Losing Colonial Venture,* summed up the opinion of many people when he wrote: "Curaçao will in time be obliged to yield to the inevitable and take the place that her geographic position and climatic conditions have ordained—a lonely island, with little political or commercial importance, and a small and poor population. During the transition from the unstable political and social conditions of a new continent, with its temporary lack of geographic adjustment, to those of social and political stability, Curaçao assumed an importance which will, with the progress of civilization and political integrity on the continent, soon be little more than a memory."

The Renaissance of the
Dutch Territories

10

The Oil Refineries of Curaçao and Aruba

T̄ʜᴇ discovery of oil in Venezuela dramatically altered the circumstances which had influenced the destiny of Curaçao for more than a century.

The Royal Dutch Shell in 1913 acquired control of the Caribbean Petroleum Company, which for several years had been investigating the possibilities of the Lake Maracaibo region. The first well was drilled in 1914, and with the presence of oil proved, the company was faced with the problems of refining and marketing.

Venezuela did not have the prospects of becoming a very large consumer of petroleum products, due to its lack of good roads and its small number of motor vehicles, nor did it appear to be a satisfactory place to build a refinery. The Maracaibo basin was hot and malarial and the fact that the entrance to Lake Maracaibo was obstructed by a bar that allowed the passage of ships drawing not more than thirteen feet of water meant that a terminus for ocean tankers would have to be built elsewhere. But there were no good harbors along the nearby Caribbean coast. Added to this, political instability within the country made the building of a refinery in Venezuela too much of a gamble for the conservative Shell interests.

Curaçao, on the other hand, had an excellent government and a good climate, and the Schottegat was capable of holding

123

an entire tanker fleet. For these reasons it was decided to build a refinery on the north side of the Schottegat near Asiento, and in 1915 the Bataafsche Petroleum Maatschappij, an operating subsidiary of the Royal Dutch Shell, started work on its construction. Operation of this refinery was begun May 23, 1918, but, due largely to inadequate shipping facilities from the oil fields, its full capacity was not reached until 1922. A subsidiary of the refining company was created in July, 1917, to cope with this shipping problem. Tank barges towed by tugboats first were used, but these proved to be both slow and unsatisfactory, and in 1919 they were replaced by shallow-draft tankers.

The Royal Dutch Shell in 1925 created a new subsidiary, the N. V. Curacaosche Petroleum Industrie Maatschappij, or C.P.I.M., to operate the Curaçao refinery, and a period of rapid expansion began. Additions to the refinery were made in 1927, and its storage capacity was increased and a new bunkering port was completed at Caracas Bay. During the next three years the plant was further enlarged and a gasoline port was built at Bullen Bay, but the 1930 world depression halted work, and for several years thereafter the output was considerably reduced. More construction preceded a destructive fire in 1936 that necessitated the virtual rebuilding of the entire plant.

Meanwhile, the Shell interests had created another subsidiary, the Arend Petroleum Maatschappij, and a small refinery had been built at Druif, Aruba, close to Oranjestad. Arend is almost wholly owned by the Mexican Eagle Oil Company—Compañia Mexicana de Petroleum "El Aguila," S.A.—which is in turn a Royal Dutch Shell subsidiary. This plant was built in 1927 because of difficulties with the Mexican Government. It has large storage facilities, but the capacity of the refinery is only about 20,000 barrels daily. It is supplied by lake tankers of the Eagle Oil and Shipping Company, Ltd., a subsidiary of the Mexican Eagle Oil Company.

The Royal Dutch Shell at first enjoyed a virtual monopoly in the Maracaibo basin, but its success invited competition, and in 1924 the Lago Oil Corporation entered the field by acquiring control of the British Equatorial Oil Company, Ltd. After studying the possibilities of a deep-water port even closer to the oil fields than Willemstad, it was decided to improve the harbor of St. Nicolaas at the southeastern end of the island of Aruba.

The Lago Transportation Company of Canada was organized to transport the oil from Lake Maracaibo to the storage tanks at St. Nicolaas, and during the last three months of 1924 almost a third of a million barrels of crude petroleum were shipped to Aruba. In 1926 and 1927 the reef protecting the southern coast of Aruba was blasted out to form an entrance to the harbor of St. Nicolaas and the harbor was dredged. The construction of a refinery with a daily capacity of 110,000 barrels of crude petroleum was begun in 1928. The following year the capacity was increased to almost 200,000 barrels daily by the construction of additional units, and the storage capacity was two million barrels.

When the refinery was finished in 1930 at a cost of eleven million dollars, it was the most completely electrically operated refinery in the world. In 1934 it superseded the C.P.I.M. refinery in Curaçao as the world's largest producer. Before the war its normal operating capacity was about a quarter of a million barrels daily, though it had passed the 300,000 barrel mark on occasions. Recent construction to increase the high octane output of both the Lago and C.P.I.M. refineries, however, has made all pre-war figures obsolete. Test runs of fuel oil at Lago have averaged as much as 325,000 barrels daily, whereas the C.P.I.M. refinery has reached a figure of 240,000 barrels daily. Ordinarily operating capacities are about 260,000 barrels and 200,000 barrels daily for the two refineries, but Venezuelan petroleum is of relatively low gravity, and as both refineries were originally designed to furnish fuel oil, when high octane gasoline is being run the daily average is much lower.

During its phenomenal growth, the control of the Lago Oil and Transport Company, Ltd., passed from the Lago Petroleum Corporation to the British Mexican Petroleum Company, Ltd., to the Pan-American Petroleum and Transport Company, to a holding company—Pan-American Eastern Corporation—to another holding company, the Lago Oil and Transport Corporation of Delaware, which was controlled by the Standard Oil Company of Indiana, and to a final holding company—the Pan-American Foreign Corporation—which is ninety-six per cent owned by the Standard Oil Company of New Jersey.

The fact that Aruba is closer to the oil fields than Curaçao makes it possible for lake tankers to average eleven round trips a month to ten for the C.P.I.M. tankers. This has also been an advantage during the war, since tankers have had to be convoyed.

The staff of the Lago refinery in May, 1943, included 705 Americans or Europeans sent from the United States, 413 staff members in the so-called intermediate group, 5,156 regular local employees, and 122 apprentices: a total of 6,396. Of these, 946 were engaged in colony service—commissary, laundry, and club and other similar occupations.

There are two groups of local employees: those from Aruba, Curaçao, and Bonaire, and others brought from Surinam, British Guiana, Jamaica, and other Caribbean islands. The locally hired staff forms the intermediate group and is recruited from the better educated islanders and occasionally from British Indians imported from British Guiana or Trinidad.

Workers in the trades and in the machine shops are almost all Arubans. Many are hired on their graduation from school and are apprenticed to the various trades. Arubans are intelligent but have not had the same constant association with mechanical things as Americans. Consequently, they must be taught their use. Apprentices are taught mathematics and mechanics and a limited amount of English, as the native language, Papiamento, is deficient in technical terms.

The wage scale for local employees at the Lago refinery varies from a basic wage of fifty-eight Dutch cents per hour for unskilled laborers to a maximum wage of 735 guilders a month for office workers or foremen. In addition to their wages, all workers receive commissary benefits. Commissary prices are adjusted from time to time to align them with prices in the United States.

There are no unions on the islands of Curaçao and Aruba, but in the Lago refinery each of the three locally hired groups has an advisory council elected by its members which represents them in discussions with company officials on all matters pertaining to working conditions.

A few years ago the average Aruban owned his own home and came to work in station wagons—the Curaçao and Aruba equivalent for busses, but the modern generation is gradually moving to St. Nicolaas and to Essoville, a colony of small houses built by the Standard Oil Company.

The oil industry employs a great number of people in both Curaçao and Aruba. There is scarcely a family on either island which is not connected either directly or indirectly with the refineries. But the local labor supply has been inadequate to supply the demands of the industry. This has been an advantage to the local people, inasmuch as the refineries are bound by an agreement with the Dutch Government to repatriate foreign employees when there is no longer work for them. There is no unemployment problem and all local employees are guaranteed a forty-eight-hour working week fifty-two weeks a year with two weeks' holiday at full pay.

There are approximately 6,000 employees in the C.P.I.M. refinery and of these 700 are Europeans. Of the remainder forty per cent are Curaçoans and sixty per cent are from the surrounding islands and from Surinam. In the last category about 200 are Portuguese from Madeira and Las Palmas. Each of these groups is paid on a different basis, and the Royal Dutch Shell prefers not to publish their wage scale, but it is common knowledge that wages in the C.P.I.M. refinery are lower than at Lago, but living costs in Curaçao are also lower.

Estimates of the basic wage in the C.P.I.M. refinery are usually about forty Dutch cents an hour, but former employees assert that the figure is much lower—less than a guilder a day.

It is unquestionably true that the low wages of the local employees contrasted with the high salaries of the European officials, who receive far more in both money and in extra benefits than even Government officials, is one of the most disturbing factors in Curaçao's economy.

It is equally true that the oil companies wield great political influence due to their contributions in taxes and to the fact that they are the largest employers and the largest importers. It is common to hear the expression, "The Government is run by the oil companies." While their power is partly justified, it has not always been wielded wisely, and the feeling of many Curaçaoans, though tempered by their realization of the benefits brought by oil, is nevertheless that of resentment.

Phosphate of lime is Curaçao's natural resource, and whereas it was discovered in 1875 by a Mr. John Godden, the deposit was only worked in a desultory fashion until after the first World War.

The property of the Curaçao Phosphate Company—Mijn-maatschappij Curaçao—is situated at Newport, on Fuik Bay. The deposit consists of rock phosphate in limestone and it occurs on the side of a flat-topped hill called Tafelberg.

The origin of the deposit would seem to be an alteration of limestone by phosphoretic acids leached out from overlaying beds of guano. This guano, of which nothing now remains, was probably laid down at sea level on the shores of a lagoon, and at a much later time the entire island was raised several hundred feet. It was at this time that weathering brought about the alteration of the limestone, which accounts for the deposit being more than 300 feet above sea level and on the side of a hill.

The quarry extends for more than a mile along the face of Tafelberg. The rock is blasted and the phosphate is sorted out in the quarry and is loaded by hand into small narrow-gauge cars and brought to the eastern end of the quarry, where it is lowered by cable railway to the plant on the shore of Fuik Bay. Here it is reduced to about three-inch size and is loaded directly onto ships which tie up to the Company's wharf, by means of a boom with an endless belt.

The Curaçao Phosphate Company also supplies the local market with lime and limestone aggregate.

Before the war most of Curaçao's phosphate was exported to the Netherlands, Germany, and the Scandinavian countries. But since 1940 almost the entire production has been shipped to England for the manufacture of superphosphate or for direct application to the soil in a finely ground condition.

The value of phosphate exports is small compared with that of petroleum, but in good years the Curaçao Phosphate Company has employed as many as 500 men and has grossed nearly a million guilders. In 1941 phosphate exports exceeded 100,000 metric tons.

The oil industry has greatly increased the shipping of Willemstad, which in 1930 surpassed both Amsterdam and Southampton in the number of ships and the gross tonnage cleared during the year. In 1941 10,000 ships of 40,000,000 tons entered the harbor. Of these, 4,000 ships, totaling 15,000,000 tons, were tankers. But this figure does not reflect the total influence of the oil industry, for much of the vastly increased tonnage is due to freight comprising refinery equipment, the increased importation of foodstuffs, and the greater demand for consumer goods due to the additional earning power of the population, which has improved the living standards and has brought the per capita imports to the highest of any Caribbean island.

In the past thirty years the population of Curaçao has doubled and that of Aruba has tripled. Willemstad has grown tremendously and the thickly populated districts now extend around the Schottegat. The refineries form a prominent part of the landscape, and Curaçao is crisscrossed by pipelines from Bullen Bay to Caracas Bay.

The C.P.I.M. refinery is a maze of pipelines leading from the piers to the storage tanks and to the cracking and topping plants. Expansion loops and pipes carried over intersections, rows of huge valves, and the confused outlines of the stacks and towers give a fantastic, dreamlike quality to the scene.

The wind grips at the towers, tearing at the steel, which shudders under the impact. The refinery is lost in a blue haze in which the light, dimly reflected from the aluminum surfaces of tanks, and the flame of burning gases become a smoky red, like a sunset seen through dark clouds close to the horizon.

The Lago refinery is so efficient that, as a result of simplification and improved methods, some of the fantastic quality of the C.P.I.M. refinery is missing. But both refineries appear deserted. Here and there a truck loaded with workers moves slowly through roads that parallel the complex of pipes, and a little group of men repairs an imperfect joint, but most of the activity is concentrated in the machine shops, the power plants, and at the piers. Elsewhere, technology has replaced men with machines.

The petroleum industry has struck the final blow to the agriculture of Curaçao and Aruba. Periodical dry spells had already forced the plantation owners to replace cattle with goats, and most of the orange trees had been killed by drought. Raising rabbits and chickens and burning charcoal were subsidiary activities, but the income to the plantations from all sources is small, plantation wages are necessarily much lower than those of the refineries, and work on the plantations still carries with it the stigma of slavery in the minds of some people. As a result, agriculture on the islands has been virtually abandoned.

Bonaire and the Windward Islands have also been affected, and their economy has been unbalanced by the emigration of the youngest and strongest members of their communities to the refineries. The only hope of improving conditions lies in the development of agriculture and animal husbandry, in the hope that they will be able to supply a part of the food of Curaçao and Aruba, but this will require a long program of readjustment and experimentation before any permanent results will have been achieved.

The future of Curaçao is bound up with the future of the oil industry, and misgivings are often expressed by Government officials because the island is dependent for its prosperity upon the raw material of another country. Theoretically, Venezuela is in a position to cut off most of Curaçao's supplies of crude petroleum and also to seriously dislocate its shipping by refusing to import or export goods through Willemstad. The latter, in fact, once occurred and was the cause of a diplomatic break between the two countries. With the stabilization of government in Venezuela, the prospect of this recurring is negligible.

Mexican expropriations of the properties of foreign oil companies were based on the exploitation of Mexican resources for which Mexico received no real benefit. Venezuela, however, has profited greatly through increased revenues and from the fact that the oil companies have explored a large part of the country and have built roads and opened up remote districts. Venezuela's satisfaction was expressed this year by the revalidation of Royal Dutch Shell and Standard Oil Company leases in the Lake Maracaibo region. The new contracts run for about forty years.

Refining is a highly technical process, and it is doubtful that, even if Venezuela wished to break its contracts, it could compete against companies with years of technological experience and great facilities for marketing their products.

The Lake Maracaibo fields have tremendous oil reserves which have scarcely been touched, and the outlook for the Curaçao and Aruba refineries from this source is excellent.

11

Bauxite and Agriculture in Surinam

I⊤ is not known exactly when bauxite was first discovered in Surinam, but the Aluminum Company of America first manifested interest in the Surinam bauxite deposits in 1915, the same year that the Royal Dutch Shell began the construction of the refinery that was to revolutionize life in Curaçao. Investigation of the deposits in British Guiana had been made two years earlier, but the Aluminum Company subsequently sold all of its foreign concessions with the exception of those in Surinam, and the British Guiana deposits are now worked by the Demerara Bauxite Company, which is incorporated in Canada. Exploration for bauxite in the jungle is difficult, but it was made easier because the deposits generally occur in low hills, due to the fact that the bauxite clay is harder and has consequently weathered less than the surrounding soil. These outcroppings were discovered by climbing tall trees to obtain an uninterrupted view of the jungle. Fortunately some of the richest deposits were accessible to the navigable rivers close to the coast.

In order to operate its concessions in Surinam, the Aluminum Company of America created the Surinam Bauxite Company— Surinaamsche Bauxiet Maatschappij—a subsidiary. It now works two deposits, one at Moengo and the other at Paranam.

Moengo was selected as the site of the first operations, as it

was considered to be the most advantageously situated, because a large deposit extends to the banks of the Cottica River,
and the mill and pier are built on mined-out areas, whereas at
Paranam the ore must be transported about four miles to the
Surinam River.

Moengo is 104 miles from Paramaribo by river, yet it is only
twenty miles from the sea due to the westerly tendency of
Surinam's rivers close to the coast. A bar at the mouth of the
Commewijne River limits the draft of ships on the Commiwijne
and Cottica rivers to seventeen feet, whereas ships drawing
nineteen feet of water can ascend the Surinam River as far
as Paranam.

There is little traffic on the river, an occasional Bush Negro
corial, a raft of hardwood being floated down to Paramaribo, or
a barge piled high with produce rowed by British Indians. The
banks are a seemingly impenetrable mass of mangroves, but
here and there a half-hidden canoe indicates a trail leading off
into the swampy brush, and at intervals the ship passes the
mouths of creeks, which run north into the ocean. Further up
the stream there are a few Bush Negro and Amerindian villages,
and as the river grows narrower and deeper the color changes
from *café au lait* to a pale gray-green, but nowhere is the water
clear.

After dark the pilot must steer by instinct, for there is little
to distinguish the wall of the jungle from the blackness of the
river. Occasionally the ship brushes the foliage on either bank.

It is late when the lights of Moengo come into view. Long
plumes of coral-colored dust rise from the holds of a ship load-
ing bauxite at the pier, and huge buildings and stacks are silhou-
etted against the night sky.

Moengo looks far bigger and more imposing at night than

it does in the daytime. Though it is a town of only 2,000 people, it is divided into several distinct districts: the factory area, containing the mill, power house, machine shops, storage buildings, piers, and offices; the native village and the quarters for the European staff, together with the hospital, coöperative store, the military barracks, moving picture theater, and school; and the Javanese village, somewhat separated from the others.

The town is by necessity a self-contained unit, and produces its own electricity, has its own refrigerating plant, telephone and wireless, and its own farm and dairy; but the bulk of its supplies have to be brought from Paramaribo.

Moengo is a strange place. Bush Negro *corials* pass up and down the river, and a few hundred yards from the mill the primitive life of the jungle continues scarcely disturbed. Bush Negroes come to town to trade or visit the hospital, where they have learned that they can get excellent medical attention, yet they do not seem to be impressed with the white man or his way of life, which must be to them far more inscrutable than the mysteries of their African gods.

The first small shipments of bauxite from Moengo in 1922 were of crude ore, and it was not until three years later that the construction of a washing and drying plant was begun for the purpose of improving the grade and eliminating excess moisture in the shipments. The difficulties of building this plant were legion: every pound of materials, except limited quantities of native lumber, had to be imported into Surinam and then shipped up the river; local labor was untrained in modern steel and concrete construction and had to be instructed in every detail; the weather was continually humid and rainy; and great difficulty was at first experienced in controlling malaria. But the plant was completed in January 1927.

At Moengo the deposit averages about eleven feet in thickness and the overburden ranges from zero to ten feet. The forest is first cleared and the soil overlying the bauxite is stripped off. The mine faces are then blasted and the ore is loaded into mine cars by Diesel shovels. At the mill the cars are dumped on a heavy bar screen and the larger lumps are broken on the screen with pavement breakers. The ore is then conveyed by endless belts to the crushers and washer and is finally dried in rotary kilns that are eight feet in diameter and 120 feet long. The dried bauxite is conveyed to the storage building from the kilns and is later loaded directly onto the ships by means of a covered boom and a conveyer belt. In this way an average cargo of 2,500 tons can be loaded in five or six hours.

The waste from the washing operation is pumped into shallow diked areas and the material washed from the bauxite, called tailings, is allowed to settle, as it cannot be released into the river, for fear of the silt forming bars and interfering with navigation.

The workers at Moengo are divided in a ratio of about eight to one between natives and Javanese. There are very few British Indians employed. The natives make good machine operators and the Javanese work well as drillers.

The average wage paid to unskilled laborers several years ago was thirty Dutch cents an hour, but it is now higher, whereas the agricultural wage in Surinam is between ten and fifteen cents an hour. It is difficult, however, to make a comparison between the two wage scales, as the Aluminum Company employees also receive certain commissary privileges and in some cases free housing, light, and water, whereas agricultural workers may or may not be housed and fed in addition to their pay, and living costs differ in various parts of the country.

The Surinam Bauxite Company is reticent about giving out

figures regarding wages, but government reports indicate that an average of 200,000 guilders monthly is paid to approximately 1,700 employees; this figure, however, includes all employees, and as some receive considerably higher pay than the average unskilled laborer, it is probable that a figure of forty cents an hour is reasonably accurate.

The development of Paranam—the name is derived from a combination of Para Creek and Surinam River—dates from 1937, but construction of the mill did not begin until 1939, and the first shipment of bauxite was made in February, 1941.

The Billiton Tin Company recently entered into competition with the Aluminum Company of America and completed a plant at Onoribo, close to Paranam, during the summer of 1942. The Billiton concession, unlike those operated by the Surinam Bauxite Company, is worked by blasting and dredging the bauxite, which lies below the ground water level.

The shipping shortage in 1942 somewhat handicapped both companies, but bauxite shipments increased from 615,534 metric tons in 1940 to 1,093,764 metric tons in 1941, and Surinam today furnishes roughly sixty per cent of the bauxite used by United States industry.

When the Surinam Bauxite Company started operations the only law covering mineral rights was an old ordinance which was intended for gold mining, but operation under this ordinance proved to be unsatisfactory, and in 1939 a concession was granted to the Surinam Bauxite Company by the Government, which guaranteed the company against discriminatory taxes. The Surinam Bauxite Company, however, is merely a subsidiary of the Aluminum Company of America and sells its entire output to the parent company, and it was foreseen that it would be impossible to control the selling price; therefore, a figure was set for tax purposes of twelve guilders fifty a ton, which may be revised up or down, according to the quality of the ore.

The Surinam Government also may levy emergency taxes, war taxes, and excess-profits taxes on the Company so long as they apply equally to other businesses, but as the Surinam Bauxite Company is the only really large business in the country, the result has been that taxes paid by the Company have formed a substantial percentage of the Government's revenues during the past few years.

Bauxite is one of the most common and widely distributed of ores, and though there are many other sources of aluminum than bauxite, none are used on a large scale. There are large bauxite deposits in France, Hungary, Russia, Istria, Yugoslavia, India, Africa, the Riouw Archipelago in the Netherlands East Indies, and in North and South America. But unless the output of France and Hungary have been greatly augmented in the past three years, Surinam is probably the world's largest producer, although the output of British Guiana, which is a closely guarded secret, may be almost as high.

One of the major reasons for the development of the Surinam bauxite deposits has been to conserve the supply in the United States. The Surinam deposits are extensive and at the present rate of production the high-grade deposits will last for many years, and there is also a considerable quantity of low-grade ore that might become profitable with improved methods of extraction.

Officials of the Aluminum Company believe that the recent phenomenal increase in the use of aluminum will continue after the war, as the majority of light alloys contain a large percentage of aluminum, but it is not unlikely that aluminum in time will have strenuous competition from even lighter metals or plastics. Recently Brazil, with a large supply of cheap labor, has entered the field. In short, it would be unwise for the Surinam Government to depend entirely on bauxite production as a source of income.

Only a small fraction of the population of Surinam is employed in the bauxite industry and the people as a whole profit from bauxite only through the increased revenues of the Government. Surinam is essentially an agricultural country, but in spite of this only 150 square miles, less than 100,000 acres, of a possible cultivable area ten times as large, are under cultivation. Many once-profitable crops have entirely disappeared and plantations have been forced to shut down or to severely curtail production for lack of labor.

Tobacco, Surinam's first crop, was grown by the early traders and by the colonists who came with Lord Willoughby in 1652. It was of poor quality, however, and had the additional disadvantage of requiring a large number of field hands. After large-scale cultivation of sugar began, tobacco was forgotten until recently, when the Javanese emigrants again took up its cultivation. It has been planted in increasing quantities since 1928, and 1,424,900 kilograms were grown in 1937. This tobacco is also of poor quality, due to insufficient fermentation and improper sorting, and is fit only for local consumption. It is doubtful that even with improvement Surinam tobacco will ever be able to compete on the world market.

Much of Surinam's colorful agricultural history is woven around the cultivation of sugar, which was also introduced by Lord Willoughby. Sugar caused the worst abuses of slavery, and brought untold wealth to some and misery and death to others.

In 1780, two hundred ships loaded with sugar from Surinam were captured by the British in the brief period between the

British declaration of war and the time that the Surinam merchants were appraised of the fact. Yet in 1941, only 9,390 metric tons of sugar were exported from Surinam, only three sugar plantations were operating, and the industry managed to exist only because of a tariff that increased the price on the local market to approximately five times that quoted in Europe.

There are a number of reasons for this decline in the sugar industry. Some stem from the nineteenth century and are identical with the causes that brought about the general retrogression of the West Indian colonies; some are inherent in the soil, for the heavy clay of the polders, together with the drainage and irrigation ditches, precludes the use of agricultural machinery; some were due to bad management; some to the fall in the price of sugar on the world market since the last war; some to the lack of cheap labor and the additional work of maintaining the polders; some to diseases and pests; and some to the lack of capital. Even the by-products of sugar, rum, and molasses have very little value. In 1940 the value of bauxite exports was twenty times that of sugar. Today the difference is much greater.

Surinam faces the unpleasant fact that sugar can be profitable only if it is cultivated on a large scale. (This has been the experience in all sugar-growing countries.) Yet the Surinam soil is not suited to machine cultivation and the labor supply is entirely inadequate. It will be necessary to overcome one or the other of these obstacles if the industry is to survive.

Cacao was introduced into Surinam during Sommelsdijk's administration, but it was not planted extensively until almost a century later.

It is native to tropical America and is found in a wild state in Surinam; consequently, it is adapted to the climate and grows well, though the heavy clay soil is not ideal for its cultivation.

It has the further advantage of requiring less attention than many other crops.

By 1895 cacao had become the most valuable crop in the country, and 445,607 kilograms were exported. But witch-broom disease, which had started in the Saramacca district, had already gained considerable headway, because the planters lacked sufficient funds to prune the diseased trees. By the time that the Government took action, it was too late and witch-broom disease had already spread throughout the country. Only ten years later the average crop had been reduced by sixty per cent.

This catastrophe resulted in an investigation of the disease by Professor Gerold Stahel, the director of the Government Agricultural Experiment Station. Professor Stahel found that it could be controlled, though at considerable expense. The drought of 1926, however, destroyed the remaining bushes and the industry has never recovered. In 1940 only 109 kilograms of cacao, worth fifty-nine guilders, were exported.

The revival of the cacao industry is a desirable objective, but it is doubtful whether large-scale planting would be advisable without proper drainage and irrigation.

The cultivation of bananas appears to have been ill-considered or at best over-optimistic from the beginning. The industry owes its origin indirectly to the rapid spread of the witch-broom disease in the cacao plantations. Both the Government and the estate owners were anxious to find another crop to take the place of cacao, and it was thought that bananas would grow well in the Surinam climate. An agreement therefore was made between the Surinam Government and the United Fruit Company in 1906 which called for the delivery of 20,000 bunches of bananas a week. The yield evidently was calculated on the company's experience in Central America without any apparent effort to discover whether similar conditions existed in Surinam, and it soon was discovered that not only far more labor was involved in banana cultivation in Surinam, but that the yield was less.

Gros Michel bananas were planted, and in the first year they were affected by Panama disease, which spread rapidly and by 1908 had seriously damaged the crop. The situation had become hopeless by 1910, and in that year experiments were made with Congo bananas, which are immune to Panama disease, but the United Fruit Company considered them unmarketable in the United States, and the following year the contract between the company and the Government was broken.

Banana plantations had been subsidized by the Government in anticipation of a return out of the profits, and a considerable amount of money was lost in this venture.

The Government Agricultural Experiment Station has made further experiments with Congo bananas since 1930, but any renewal of the culture awaits the conclusion of the war. At present bananas are grown in increasing quantities for home consumption, but the exports are very small.

Arabica coffee was introduced into Surinam from Java in the beginning of the eighteenth century, and by 1730 its cultivation was widely extended. It was at that time one of the colony's most important crops, and reached its highest point between 1775 and 1800, but after the abolition of slavery, it declined, due to insufficient labor. Of 178 plantations in 1832, only thirty remained in 1873.

After the introduction of Asiatic labor into the colony, coffee was again planted in 1890, but this time the more robust Liberian coffee was tried. This crop is well adapted to the soil and the climate, though it requires shade trees because of the excessive heat. However, it is an inferior grade and its market is therefore limited.

The planting of Liberia coffee was greatly extended in 1912-1914 following the failure of the banana crop, and the remaining banana trees were used for shade. High coffee prices in 1925-1930 further stimulated the industry, but after 1930 a severe decline in prices forced several of the plantations into financial difficulties. In spite of this, Liberia coffee was the most valuable export crop in 1935, 1936, and 1939.

There is normally no market for Liberia coffee in the United States, and the Netherlands and Norway were the largest outlet for Surinam's coffee. This market was cut off by the war, and the plantations experienced great difficulties. Some have been closed and in others the production has been severely limited. In 1940 the amount exported was only one-fourth that of the preceding year, but in 1941 there was a partial recovery, due to arrangements having been made for Surinam to export 25,000 bags of coffee to the United States—a portion of the quota of the Netherlands East Indies. Further expansion of imports to the United States at this time is unlikely, due to limitations of shipping space, and a successful invasion of the United States market, moreover, would require an improvement in both the taste and the appearance of Liberian coffee. It is unfortunate that the cultivation of the more easily marketable Arabica coffee could not have been continued.

Cotton was first planted on a large scale in 1752 and became important during the British occupations between 1800 and 1816. It was grown chiefly in the Coronie District, which had recently been opened up to colonization, but with the return of Surinam to Dutch rule, and particularly with the abolition of the slave trade, the plantations were abandoned. By 1873 cotton had all but disappeared.

Attempts made to revive its culture between 1920 and 1930 on dry territories close to the sea failed completely, as the crop was attacked by stainer. Cotton, in any case, is too dependent on the weather to flourish in Surinam.

Rice was grown in increasing quantities as more and more British Indians and Javanese came to Surinam, and the first World War, with attendant high prices, further stimulated the industry. Whereas prior to the war about six million kilograms of rice were imported annually, in 1916 this figure was reduced by sixty per cent, and for the years 1938-1939 there was an annual exportable surplus of seven million kilograms. The most important rice-producing district is Nickerie.

In rice, Surinam finally appears to have found a crop that is well adapted to the soil and to the available labor supply. Both the British Indians and the Javanese have had generations of experience in its cultivation. It has become Surinam's most important crop, and its further development promises well for the future. There are, however, a few difficulties to be overcome and a few improvements that can be made. Empoldering and irrigation are essential, and already a long step forward has been made by the Government in the Nickerie District with the opening of the new Clara Polder and an irrigation canal from Nanni Creek. This will prevent a repetition of the loss incurred from the drought of 1940.

Further work must be done in educating the population in the planting of supplementary crops on the high land that is unsuitable for rice; a better understanding must be brought about between the three races engaged in planting—natives, British Indians, and Javanese—or they will have to be entirely segregated; better milling methods must be found to avoid the excessive breakage that has heretofore reduced the value of Surinam rice on the world market; and better seed is also needed to improve the quality. Progress has already been made along all of these lines, and the Government is showing a marked interest and a desire to further this most promising crop.

The export of rice was restricted by Government order in 1940 in order to conserve the food supply, and exports in 1940 and 1941 were only twenty-five per cent of those of 1939.

The recent high wages paid by United States forces in Surinam have lured many Asiatics from the polders to Paramaribo, and they have shown a reluctance to return. Consequently, the rice crop has suffered, and in the spring of 1943 there was a shortage for the first time in several years.

A large percentage of the exports had previously gone to the French islands of Guadeloupe and Martinique and to French Guiana. There is no reason why these markets should not be regained when normal export is resumed, and postwar markets in the West Indies, South America, and Europe are promising, especially if tariff barriers are lifted.

The impossibility of machine cultivation should not prove too great a handicap with an Asiatic population.

Coconut culture is almost exclusively confined to the Coronie District, where a series of sand and shell ridges rise above the surrounding swamps. These ridges are typical of the Surinam coastal plain, and their soil is lighter and the drainage better than in the polders. Coronie was once the center of the cotton industry, but today its preponderantly Negro and mulatto population grows coconuts and rice, raises pigs, and keeps bees. Coconuts grow well, and though some of the trees are affected by so-called core putrefaction, one plantation manager told me that he had had very little trouble from this source.

There are fewer labor problems in Coronie than in the other districts of Surinam due to its isolation, and several of the coconut plantations have done very well.

It is difficult to understand why coconut culture is not more widespread. There are many localities where the trees could be grown, and there should be a good market for copra. It is the old problem of protective tariffs and trade agreements that makes it cheaper to buy from markets halfway around the world than near at hand.

One of the impediments to an extension of coconut planting is the lack of communication and the expense of transportation within the country, but new roads are now being built which will help to solve the latter problem.

Increased shipping service between South America and the United States and between South America and Europe would put Surinam in a more favorable position to market its agricultural products, and if no other means are available, it will be necessary to increase shipping services by Government subsidy. This has been done in the development of the East Indies and in the case of the less important Windward Islands of the Territory of Curaçao, and it certainly should be done in Surinam.

The cultivation of citrus fruits has been expanded considerably during the past fifteen years, yet oranges and grapefruits have never become important exports. During the years 1936-1939 the value of orange exports averaged only nine thousand guilders annually.

The climate of Surinam is excellent for the cultivation of oranges, as there is generally sufficient rainfall and the temperature is even, and there is no danger of frost. Orange trees have been planted on both sandy and clay soils, though clay does not drain properly and is therefore conducive to root rot.

The appearance of Surinam oranges is against their acceptance on the United States market, but as juice-oranges they are fully as good as, if not better than, those grown in

California and Florida. Most fruit heretofore has been exported
to the Netherlands, and decay in transit has presented a problem, but it has been found that refrigeration is not necessary
if shipment is made by express service.

The Netherlands market has been destroyed by the war,
and many of the Surinam orchards have suffered from neglect
as a result. If the problem of marketing can be solved, the
future of the citrus fruit industry in Surinam, though modest,
would be assured.

Experiments with oil palm and sisal during the past twenty
years have not been encouraging, nor has the soil proved to be
suitable for the cultivation of pineapples. Peanuts are grown in
small quantities, and peanut oil is used to supplement the insufficient quantities of coconut oil produced in the country.
The cultivation of Assam tea has been suggested, but it is
doubtful whether it would grow well in the hot, moist climate
of Surinam.

Indigo, one of Surinam's earliest exports, long ago lost its
market through its replacement by synthetic dyes. Quassia bitter root—named after Quassi, a Bush Negro Granman—the
lignum quassiae Surinamense of the pharmocopeia, has been
exported very irregularly for the past hundred years, and recently it has been pushed off of the market by Jamaican bitter
root.

Finally, it is strange that bitter cassava, which is native to
Surinam, has never been exploited commercially. It is the
staple of the Bush Negro and Amerindian diet, and its export as
tapioca should be a welcome addition to Surinam's meager list
of agricultural successes.

Forest products—rubber, balata, and timber—also form a
part of Surinam's exports. Professor Stahel writes regarding

rubber, "If it were possible to furnish a species of *hevea* which resisted the South American leaf disease, the cultivation of rubber would certainly have a good chance, considering that the tree before the disease was growing very well. One finds *Hevea Brasiliensis* in the lower Amazon on a soil which apparently has a great deal in common with the clay of our plantations." Plans for large rubber plantations however will have to wait on capital and labor.

Balata, the latex of the bully tree, a substitute for gutta percha, and rubber for cable covering, insulation, and golf balls, has been exported since 1895. Exports increased until 1914, but have declined since that time. Nevertheless, balata ranks as one of Surinam's most important products. In spite of increased demands for rubber and rubber substitutes due to the war, balata exports for 1941 closely approximated those of 1938 but fell far below the figures for 1939.

The difficulties of collection and transportation have affected balata exports. There are no balata plantations, and trees in the jungle must be tapped. Ignorance and willful mistreatment of the trees, such as overbleeding in the hope of quick gain, have resulted in their destruction in the more accessible locations, and much of the latex must now be brought from far up the rivers and through the rapids by Bush Negro *corials*. Furthermore, collection of this type is most uncertain, and labor is unreliable.

Lumbering suffers from almost the same difficulties that are experienced in the collection of balata. There are the same problems of remote location, unreliability of labor, and consequent erratic delivery, and the necessity to single out individual trees. The result is that timber can be imported more cheaply than it can be brought from the interior. Every lumber company that was established in the past hundred years, even the most efficiently managed, failed for these reasons.

A certain amount of timber is floated down the rivers by

the Bush Negroes every year for local consumption, and limited quantities of pile wood, *basra locus, dicorynia paraensis,* mora, letterwood, and purpleheart are exported, but there are hundreds of different hard woods in the Surinam jungle and lumbering will not pay so long as only a few kinds are in demand.

Animal industry in Surinam suffers from its characteristic defects in all tropical countries. Tropical diseases and improper forage result in lean cattle that yield poor beef and small quantities of milk, and slaughtering and refrigeration facilities are inadequate. The British Indians are the chief cattle raisers, and the Dutch farmers provide some competition. Pigs do very well at Coronie and could probably be raised in other districts, but due to insufficient home production, Surinam imports much of its meat.

To summarize: Surinam's agricultural difficulties have arisen from the limitation of crops by topography and climate; the excessive cost of clearing the fields and keeping them clear of the encroaching jungle; the necessity of building polders with drainage and irrigation canals; the fact that machine cultivation is impractical, if not impossible, in the clay soils of the polders; the lack of good roads and the impracticability of building them; the lack of proper shipping facilities between Surinam, North America, South America, and Europe; the lack of sufficient capital to tide the plantations over periods of low prices and wars; the barrier of preferential tariffs in the other countries, especially in the British Antilles; the fact that there has not been an aggressive marketing program; the lack of an adequate labor supply and the consequent high wage scale; and, finally, plant diseases.

The difficulty has been to discover a crop which will grow well, which is immune to disease, which can be cultivated with the available labor, and for which there is a market.

Today and Tomorrow

12

Government

THE government of the Nether-
lands West Indies islands in its initial stage was marked by many
disagreements and changes of policy. In theory, at least, the
Dutch West India Company was given the responsibility for all
lands in the Western Hemisphere, but in 1628, only seven years
after the founding of the Company, it was decided to divide the
responsibility between the different provinces of the Netherlands. Amsterdam was given the government of New Netherland, and a few years later of Curaçao, Aruba, and Bonaire;
whereas Zeeland controlled Essequebo and during the Second
Anglo-Dutch War captured Surinam from the British.

The smaller islands of St. Martin, Saba, and St. Eustatius,
together with Berbice, were at first indirectly administered by
the West India Company and were later governed by Zeeland,
and after 1773 by Rotterdam.

Between 1647 and 1664 Curaçao was united with New
Netherland under the governorship of Peter Stuyvesant, but
when New Netherland was captured by the English, Curaçao
again was given its own administration.

Zeeland in 1682 sold Surinam to the West India Company,
which in turn sold interests of one-third each to the van Aerssen
family and the City of Amsterdam, and a new company was

formed which was incorporated as the Chartered Society of Surinam.

Surinam and Curaçao, with the other Dutch islands, came under the States General in 1791 when the Dutch West India Company was finally dissolved, but the French Revolution and the Napoleonic wars resulted in their changing hands several times before they were returned to Holland in 1816. Control of the colonies now rested with the States General and they were administered under the new Constitution of the Netherlands of 1815.

Curaçao and Surinam both had suffered during the wars, and in 1828 it was decided to place them under one governor, but as communications were poor this resulted in unnecessary delays in administration, and in 1845 they were again separated and each colony received its own governor.

With all of these changes, and with the conflicting policies represented by the different cities and governments, confusion was bound to result. Furthermore, the interests of the Dutch West India Company were opposed to those of the colonies, and the governors, or, more properly, the directors sent out by the Company were paid as little as twelve hundred guilders annually, with an allowance of one thousand guilders for expenses, so it is not surprising that they should seek other ways of making money, to the detriment of both colony and Company interests. Added to this, communication with Europe by sailing ship was necessarily slow, and it often took many months, or even years, to replace incompetent directors or to correct policies which had proved detrimental to all concerned.

Until 1922 the administration of Curaçao and Surinam was based on the Regeeringsreglement, or Fundamental Colonial Law, drawn up in 1865 which in turn was based on the Netherlands Constitution. The establishment of a Koloniale Raad, or

Colonial Council, in Surinam and Curaçao, giving to each colony a certain measure of autonomy, dates back to the institution of this Fundamental Colonial Law.

In 1922 both the Netherlands Constitution and the colonial law were revised, and the status of the colonies was formally changed to that of Territories. The new Constitution states that anyone within the Territories is entitled to freedom of person, freedom of union and meeting, and freedom of petition; and it guarantees freedom of the press.

Each Territory is administered by a Governor appointed by the Crown who is directly responsible to the Crown. The Governor may be either a citizen of Holland or of the Territories. He is assisted by an Advisory Council, the Raad van Bestuur, of which the Governor is president, and to which a vice-president and three other members are regularly appointed by the Crown. Under the new Constitution extraordinary members may also be appointed. The capacity of the Raad is purely advisory, but it must be consulted for all regulations, by-laws, decrees of the Governor, budgets, and acts.

A second council, formerly the Koloniale Raad, now the Staten, is composed of fifteen members, five of whom are appointed by the Governor after consultation with the Raad van Bestuur, and ten are elected. The ordinances of the Governor and the budget are submitted to the Staten, which has the right to amend them.

Voters in Curaçao number only about five per cent of the population, and in Surinam one to one and one-half per cent of the population.

According to the new suffrage regulations of 1937, the right to vote in Surinam can be exercised only by those who are male Netherlands subjects; are legally resident in Surinam since January 1 of the year of election; have attained the age of twenty-five; enjoy full civil rights; are either assessed for taxes on the basis of a minimum annual income of eight hundred guilders; or who meet certain educational standards. The requirements of a voter in Curaçao are similar to those of Surinam. The franchise does not extend to women, though they can be elected to office.

Members of the Staten serve for a period of four years and resign as a body at the end of that time. Each year the president and vice-president are chosen from among its members by the Governor. The Secretary of the Staten is elected by the members but cannot be one of them.

Government departments include Attorney General, Government Secretary, Finances, Public Works, Public Health, Social and Economic Affairs, Education, Customs, Post Office, Police, and Fire.

The island of Curaçao is divided into three districts: Willemstad, eastern Curaçao, and western Curaçao. At the head of each are District-Meesters, who are directly responsible to the Governor.

Aruba and Bonaire are administered by Gezaghebbers, or Lieutenant Governors, who are responsible to the Governor in Curaçao, and each is assisted by two Landraden, or Local Councilors, who are elected for alternating terms of two years apiece. The Gezaghebber and Landraden together form the Raad van Politie, or Police Council, which acts in an advisory capacity to the Governor in all local matters.

St. Martin, like Aruba and Bonaire, is governed by a Gezaghebber, and Saba and St. Eustatius are administered by Onder-Gezaghebbers responsible to him.

The Court of Justice for the Territory of Curaçao consists of a Chief Justice and five other members established at Willemstad. Both civil and criminal cases are tried by a Judge, and an appeal is decided by the Chief Justice and two members of the court, neither of whom has previously tried the case. No appeal can be made to a higher court in Holland.

One of the five Justices is installed on Aruba and deals with all cases on the island, but the islands of Bonaire, St. Martin, Saba, and St. Eustatius are visited periodically by one of the Justices who decides all cases beyond the jurisdiction of the local administrator.

Courts-martial are conducted by a Justice of the regular court acting as president and one army and one navy officer.

The police force is divided into three corps; the Military Police, the Civil Police, and the Rural Constabulary.

The Military Police is responsible for street patrol and traffic duty in Willemstad and the eastern part of the island of Curaçao and for the entire island of Aruba. It is also in charge of the Fire Brigade on both Aruba and Curaçao. Most of its personnel are from the Netherlands.

The Civil Police does harbor duty and is in charge of the Aliens Office, Passport Control Office, and detective and investigation work. It draws a large part of its personnel from the Military Police.

The Rural Constabulary, consisting mostly of natives, is in charge of police work in the western half of Curaçao and on the islands of Bonaire, St. Martin, Saba, and St. Eustatius.

A factor that must be considered in relation to the Government of Curaçao is the influence exerted by the Catholic Church. The roots of Catholicism go very deep in the Leeward Islands, for they were planted by the Spaniards more than a century before the Dutch conquest of the islands, and since 1705 Catholic missionaries of various nations, Jesuits, Franciscans, and others, have been continually at work. They were the more successful because many Protestant landholders, wishing to emphasize the distinction between themselves and their slaves, had the slave children christened as Catholics, and neither at this time nor subsequently did the Protestant Church make any effort to promote their faith. The result has been that about seventy-five per cent of the population is today Catholic.

There has been a gentlemen's agreement since 1909 that all governors of Curaçao be Catholics and governors of Surinam be Protestants. But there has been some dissatisfaction over this policy in recent years, as a large percentage of the European population of Curaçao is Protestant and the most influential families on the island are Jews, and it is probable that it will be abandoned after the war.

Catholic influence in the schools is even greater than the number of Catholics on the islands would indicate, and in 1938 fully ninety per cent of the school children attended Catholic schools.

The majority of the schools in the Territory are primary schools, but education is carried through a grade that corresponds roughly to the last year of high school in the United States. There are several technical schools in Curaçao and between eight and ten per cent of the revenues of the Territory are spent on education.

The Government of Curaçao, in Venezuela, prior to the discovery of oil, was largely in the hands of a few influential island families, but the promise of profits brought with it a renewal of interest by the Netherlands. It suddenly was discovered that the Curaçaoans were not capable of managing their own affairs, and a greater number of officials were sent out from Holland. There was some justification in this move, for the problems of government became infinitely more complicated, but it has inevitably resulted in a certain amount of resentment among the local population, and it is desirable that, wherever possible, Government offices be returned to the Curaçaoans, who not only have a clearer understanding of their own problems, but also have a natural desire to govern themselves.

The rapid increase in the population of Aruba and its industrialization have brought with them a demand for increased representation in the government of Curaçao and in the Netherlands Council as well.

The Windward Islands pose a question, for although the present system of government through Curaçao works well in many respects, it is open to the criticism that the central government is not always well-informed regarding local problems and that the administrators are not given enough authority. The problems differ greatly from those of the A B C islands, and many people believe that their affairs are not given sympathetic consideration. A movement was started a few years ago that put forward the idea that the Windward Islands be governed separately from Curaçao, but this is entirely impractical. Much of the difficulty unquestionably arises from the fact that the Windward Islands represent a four hundred thousand guilder a year drain upon the Curaçao budget.

Government in the Windward Islands has been by halfway measures that have been unsatisfactory alike to Curaçao and to the Windward Islanders. People still have to walk long distances to find water, and there is not enough for the cattle. Agriculture also is severely handicapped by recurrent droughts and without proper irrigation will probably never be able to compete with islands that are better supplied with water. It would be possible to dig artesian wells or to construct hillside catchment surfaces, as in Bermuda and the Virgin Islands, yet only a few shallow wells have been dug. Likewise, the Government has spent some money in improving the salt ponds, but unless they are completely modernized, competition with the up-to-date installations on the neighboring British island of Anguilla will be impossible.

There is now a Government Agricultural Experiment Station on St. Martin, and several attempts have been made to introduce a better breed of cattle, but the effort has fallen short of its mark because of inexperience, lack of understanding of the problem in Curaçao, and insufficient funds. The Government will have to make up its mind either to spend money over a period of several years on a program of education of the people and for experiments by an experienced agronomist, or else abandon the project altogether, for the present compromise methods amount to nothing more than throwing good money after bad. Similarly, the present policy of no taxes, low tariffs, and free transportation of goods on the Government-subsidized steamer from the Windward Islands to Curaçao, though signifying an unselfish attitude on the part of the Government, has been shown to have its disadvantages. There is a growing tendency on the part of the people to take advantage of the situation, a natural result of their having no responsibilities, and this will inevitably result in widespread pauperism.

When communications between the Leeward and Windward groups are improved, it will make for better understanding, and many of the present difficulties can be avoided.

The Government of Surinam differs little from that of Curaçao. The country is divided into seven districts, each administered by a District Commissioner, who is directly responsible to the Governor, and who is also in charge of the police in his district.

The highest judicial body is the Court of Justice at Paramaribo. There are also district courts in Paramaribo, Nickerie,

Coronie, and Marowijne, and Justices travel in the other districts.

Education in Surinam has been compulsory since 1876 for children between the ages of seven and twelve, except for the Javanese and British Indian immigrants and the Bush Negroes and Amerindians living in the jungle. There are, however, several missionary schools among the primitive tribes, and recently two experimental *desa* schools, patterned after those in Java, have been started.

Only one-third of the pupils in Surinam go to Catholic schools, another third attend Government schools, and the remaining third are divided between Moravian, Baptist, and African Methodist Episcopal schools.

There are four classes of schools: restricted, elementary, continuation, and high schools, and in addition there are several vocational schools.

The government in Surinam is top-heavy and has been hampered by a ridiculously small budget, amounting to only six or seven million guilders a year in ordinary times and to less than ten million guilders at the present time. It is only half that of Curaçao. In spite of this, deficits of from two to three million guilders annually have resulted in a strict control of Surinam finances by the Netherlands Government, and while this is necessary, it is noteworthy that neither Surinam nor Curaçao are represented in the States General. Representation, however, has been promised following the war.

The problem of governing so many different races—Negroes, British Indians, Javanese, Chinese, Bush Negroes, and Amerindians—of so many different religions—Christian, Mohammedan, Hindu, Confucian, and Animist—is a difficult one. An attempt has been made to rule the people according to their own beliefs, rather than to impose European laws upon them. An offense committed by a Javanese is punished according to the dictates of his national *adat,* or law, which is different than the treatment accorded a similar action by a British Indian or a Negro.

This type of government demands a tremendous amount of education in the customs of the various peoples and a broad understanding and sympathy on the part of the administrator. For this reason, a District Commissioner in Surinam should have an even wider training than his counterpart, the Resident or Assistant-Resident in the Netherlands East Indies.

Unfortunately, the policy applied to the West Indies has been different from that in the East. Whereas civil servants destined for Java are trained in the Netherlands for several years in the languages, religion, and *adat* of the country, no such qualifications are required of the West Indian administrator. In fact, many civil servants trained for the East Indies, or those who have already been to the East, are sent to Surinam and Curaçao without regard to the fact that not only the problems, but the people and their outlook, are entirely different.

For these reasons the West Indies suffer a feeling of territorial inferiority, and the people have developed an "East Indies complex." Opportunities in the West Indies are less than in the East, and the East Indies official compares everything with his previous experience, to the detriment of the West. Many officials consequently, come to believe that, because not all things are possible, nothing is possible, and that they cannot be efficient in the West Indies, so they make no further effort.

I recall asking the commissioner at Moengo if he didn't have a car. "Yes," he replied, "I have three cars and two launches, but unfortunately none of them are working." Another time I remarked to a high Government official that I should think things might be arranged a little more efficiently, and to emphasize my point, I said, "If the Governor were going on a trip,

Schooners at Oranjestad, Aruba.

Patriarch of Simsons Bay, St. Martin.

Fisherman of Slagbaai, Bonaire.

U.S. Troops Guard the Lago Refinery.

St. Nicolaas Harbor, Aruba.

Drying Fish Nets, St. Eustatius.

Landing Place at St. Eustatius.

Coming Ashore at Fort Bay, Saba.

Careenage at Oranjestad, Aruba.

Salt Works, Bonaire.

Baling Hay, St. Martin.

Ruins of Salt Works, St. Martin.

Fort Amsterdam, St. Martin.

Philipsburg—between Bay and Salt Ponds.

Boat Building at Kralendijk.

Aloe Field, Bonaire.

Mountain Trail on Saba.

Aruban Soldier.

Ruins of Dutch Reformed Church, St. Eustatius.

Negro-Indian Woman of Bonaire.

I imagine that someone would see that everything were in order, instead of waiting for a launch or an automobile to break down." His reply was typical. "You evidently don't understand Surinam." "But I have been in more remote spots than this in the East Indies," I countered, "and I never had the slightest difficulty." His reply was most typical of all: "Yes, but the East Indies are different."

The Netherlands Government alone is not at fault in this, because even ambitious Curaçaoans and Surinamers prefer the greater opportunities of the East to the hard work of improving conditions in their own Territories.

13

Effects of the War

COINCIDENT with the invasion of Holland on May 10, 1940, martial law was proclaimed in the Netherlands West Indies, and the colonial councils of Surinam and Curaçao declared war on Germany. Ten German ships in the harbors of Curaçao and Aruba were seized after efforts to scuttle several of them were frustrated, and their crews were interned on Bonaire. But German seamen later were transferred to Jamaica for internment, and only those Germans who had been residents of Curaçao were kept in Bonaire.

In Paramaribo the German merchant ship *Goslar* was scuttled while officials were waiting to take the crew ashore. It still lies on its side in the middle of the Surinam River but fortunately does not interfere with navigation.

British troops of the King's Shropshire Light Infantry were immediately dispatched from Jamaica to Curaçao to protect the C.P.I.M. refinery, and French marines landed on Aruba, but a few weeks later, when France made peace with Germany, the marines were replaced by a Scottish regiment.

The war brought with it only a brief flurry of excitement, which soon died down. Life in Curaçao was little changed. There was still no thought of danger to the West Indies.

The internment camp at Bonaire is on the beach close to Kralendijk. The Germans and Dutch Nazis are segregated. The women with children have been given small individual houses and the men with wives and families are permitted to visit them. The possibility of allowing the men to live with their families was being discussed in the spring of 1942.

Bonaire has an excellent climate and the prisoners are all fat and healthy, testifying to the excellent treatment that they have received. They are allowed to play football and to swim and, whenever possible, to follow their hobbies. In spite of this, they complain constantly, and several of them jokingly intimated to me that I was being shown only the good side of the camp. Their attitude of bravado was proof enough that they had nothing to complain about.

Several months after visiting Bonaire, I had an opportunity to talk with the Swiss Consul from Caracas, who periodically inspects the camps in Bonaire and Surinam, and he concurred with my observations.

German Jews and anti-Nazis were released from the camp a year and a half ago, though they must remain on the island.

An attempt by four men to escape from the camp on Bonaire was unsuccessful as they were intercepted by a plane when only a few miles from the Venezuelan coast. Two similar attempts at escape from the internment camp near Paramaribo have also resulted in the recapture of the prisoners.

In the spring of 1940, with the European situation becoming increasingly serious, discussions were begun between the Governments of the Netherlands and the United States, with a view to strengthening the defenses of Surinam. Many militarists believed that it was only a matter of time before England gave up the war; the French colonies were controlled by Germany through the Vichy Government; and the possibility of an invasion of South America by way of Dakar seemed a distinct possibility.

Had the Netherlands Government been willing to detach Dutch troops in England for duty in Surinam, it would not have been necessary for the United States to intervene, but the Dutch wanted to have every man available in England when the time came to drive the Germans out of Holland.

It was distasteful to the Territories to have to accept help even from an ally, and they demurred, but the training of native troops had just begun, and it would have been impossible for them to handle the complicated machinery of modern war.

The first United States troops landed in Surinam on November 25, at a time when the United States and the Netherlands were engaged in delicate diplomatic negotiations with Japan and when the situation in the Pacific was becoming increasingly tense. But if this move was intended to impress Japan with Dutch-American unity, this was a secondary consideration, for negotiations had long been under way. As a demonstration of hemisphere solidarity, it could have carried little conviction, for Brazil's participation was negligible, though the move was made with the knowledge of the Latin-American countries.

The force sent to Surinam was ridiculously small and ill-equipped, but at that time the troops and material that could be spared were limited. There were too few planes, and these few were often grounded for lack of parts. The number of troops provided no adequate defense, and it was to be amply proved in Malaya that the jungle is no barrier to an invasion. The same fact had been equally well proved one hundred and fifty years earlier in Surinam during the slave insurrections.

The intentions of the Government of French Guiana were eyed with suspicion, because the bauxite plant at Moengo was only a few kilometers from the French Guiana border. At Moengo-Tapoe a few experienced soldiers from Java coöperated with Bush Negroes in training troops in jungle warfare, but this training was carried out on a small scale.

Had Surinam been isolated, a force to be effective would have had to be at least ten times as large and to have had far better equipment. But Surinam can be considered as one of a chain of bases, supported by others in Brazil, British Guiana, and Trinidad.

The number of troops in the country has since been increased and their equipment materially improved. Many native troops, furthermore, are now fully trained.

Coöperation between the United States forces and the Surinam Government has been excellent from the beginning, in spite of the initial objections to American participation in the defense of the Territory; and everywhere officials have expressed the opinion that, so long as it was necessary to bring in an outside force, it could not have been accomplished with more tact than was done by the United States Army.

American troops are little in evidence in Paramaribo, and are extraordinarily well behaved, considering the uneventful life that they are forced to lead at Zanderij, Paranam, and Moengo. The same, however, cannot be said for the employees of construction companies under contract to the army to build roads, camps, and airports.

In January, 1942, it was decided to send United States troops to Curaçao to relieve the British garrison. The equipment of the British troops was hopelessly inadequate and consisted of .30-caliber machine guns and trench mortars, with a few Bren gun carriers. The Dutch troops had even less equipment. There were a few coast defense guns, but no anti-aircraft protection and no air force, unless the Dutch Army's thirteen-year-old Fokker could be considered as one. The Navy consisted of one cruiser and two trawlers, but in the fall of 1941 six motor torpedo boats were brought to Curaçao from Canada to be fitted for duty in the East Indies. By December it was obvious to anyone who knew anything about the situation in the East that they would not arrive in time, and they were transferred to the West Indies command and are now doing patrol and convoy duty in the waters around the Leeward Islands.

There was never any question of an invasion of Curaçao or Aruba, but a commando attack by forces brought in by submarine, or even shelling from the sea, could have crippled the refineries at a time when they were all-important. The possibility of either contingency, however, had been discounted, and it was not until the summer of 1941 that 2,700,000 guilders had finally been appropriated for defense of the Netherlands West Indies, but by that time there was no equipment to be had.

The British soldiers were bored with the monotony of continuous guard duty, and their officers were universally anxious to return to England to active service. They also were in the unenviable position of knowing that, if any serious attempt were made on the refineries, they would be able to do very little to prevent it. Furthermore, there was always a certain amount of friction between the British and the Dutch, both among the officers and the men; nothing serious, but trivialities that would not have occurred had there been anything more important to think about. British officers claimed that the Dutch refused to cooperate in developing methods of defense, and that they were charged an exorbitant rent for the use of their barracks. The Dutch countered that British troops were continually starting fights in Willemstad.

The vanguard of the American forces, a small number of air-force personnel and three medium bombers, arrived in the middle of January. This was the first time that Curaçao had had air protection. The main American forces, however, did not arrive until February 12, and four days later German submarines struck at the refineries of Curaçao and Aruba and at the vulnerable lake tankers for the first time in an attempt to cut off vital supplies of oil and high-octane gasoline from reaching the British forces in England and North Africa. But the attack was ill-conceived, and there was a feeling in official circles that originally it had been aimed at the transports, and that the subsequent attack on the refineries was an improvisation.

Several lake tankers were torpedoed close to Aruba, and at St. Nicolaas torpedoes crashing into tankers at the pier spread masses of flaming oil across the harbor. Shells subsequently were fired at point-blank range from the deck guns of the submarines, but the aim of the gunners was obscured by the smoke and flame, and the submarines were driven off before they could do any real harm. The only damage to the refinery was a dent in a storage tank. A few shells also passed harmlessly through the roofs of houses in the residential section.

This attack came when the refinery was fully lighted and before American guns had been placed, and it would be impossible to repeat it. A submarine, attempting to shell the C.P.I.M. refinery in Curaçao a few weeks later, was forced to crash-dive after firing only two or three shots, and for the past year neither refinery has been attacked.

The immediate results of the submarine attack on the islands was that a blackout replaced the occasional air-raid drills of the previous months. It lent authenticity to the war. The legend of safety had been exploded.

The balcony of the Hotel Americano was no longer a scene of gaiety at night. Now there were blackout shutters, and people congregated inside at the bar. On moonless nights there was a certain inconvenience in traveling from place to place on the island, but it was not an impossibility. The blackout brought a suggestion of mystery to Willemstad. In the moonlight the buildings seemed luminous from the reflected light and here and there glowed with a suggestion of color, that was repeated by suppressed glimmers of light coming from doorways and windows and leading back into the deep recesses of houses, where people sat about shaded lamps in inner rooms. Curaçao seemingly had turned back the clock one hundred years.

The second immediate result of the submarine warfare was that all lake tankers were ordered into port, and there was a strike of tanker crews. Many captains refused to sail until emergency life-saving equipment was installed on their ships. But the Government and the oil companies took the attitude that the oil must be brought to the refineries at all costs for their storage capacity is only equal to about a week's supply. They promised to equip the ships as rapidly as possible, but insisted that meanwhile the tankers be taken out in convoy.

There was no lack of patriotism among the seamen, but if a man is to risk his life, he is at least entitled to ask that everything be done to improve his chances. It also was obvious that the flow of oil to the battlefields of Europe should not be stopped. There was justification for the attitude of both sides, but the real fault lay in the lack of previous preparation and foresight.

The present war has left a definite mark on the economy of the Netherlands West Indies.

The reduction of shipping perhaps has had the greatest effect on the territory of Curaçao, for during the past twenty-five years the refineries of Curaçao and Aruba have drawn their employees from the agricultural workers of the islands, and the high wages paid in the refineries has encouraged the people to stop growing food, even for their own use, as they can afford imported foodstuffs. Furthermore, the population of both islands greatly increased, and it is improbable that even if agriculture were encouraged, it would be adequate to support the present population.

Prior to the war, almost all food for Aruba, and to a lesser extent for Curaçao, was imported from the United States, but recently vegetables and fruit have been brought from Venezuela. A new road net, built by the Government through the mountains north of the Maracaibo basin, has opened up country in which almost any vegetable that is grown in the United States can be raised. Consequently, produce is now available that would previously have spoiled on the way to market due to transportation difficulties.

The decrease in the output of oil following the first torpedoings has been succeeded by a new program of modernization and by greatly accelerated production in both the C.P.I.M. and Lago refineries.

Rising prices due to the normal effects of war scarcity are to be expected, but on the arrival of United States troops in Curaçao prices soared. Where in January, 1942, I had paid ten guilders a day for a station wagon and driver, the identical car and driver cost me twenty-five guilders a day in March. Hotel accommodations also had risen twenty to twenty-five per cent in the same period.

The American soldiers had plenty of money and their sense of values had not been adjusted to Caribbean living standards. They were as eagerly welcomed by the shopkeepers as the tourists who had formerly thronged Herrenstraat.

The American soldiers were much more in evidence than the British had been, and I know that most Curaçaoans had not looked forward to their coming. Yet, after they had been on the island for a few weeks, they were well liked for their enthusiasm and their efficiency as well as for their money. But the fact that they receive higher pay than the Dutch troops makes for bad feeling. This is the same problem that is being encountered in all parts of the world at the present time, but it seems reasonable to suggest that the pay of American troops in foreign countries in excess of the amount paid to the troops of the country that they are garrisoning be withheld until their return to the United States. It would also make for better relations if entertainers coming to a small island like Curaçao to perform for the Americans also could spare the time to perform for the local forces.

Changes made by the Americans have proved welcome to the local people in one respect. Restaurants and hotels in Curaçao were declared out of bounds for army and navy men until they met certain standards approved by the Medical Corps. Most Curaçaoans consider this to be a good step, and I was told by one Government official that more had been accomplished in a month in this way than could have been gained by legislation in ten years.

In 1941 the Government in Surinam, in order to conserve dollar reserves, instituted a system of quotas which severely reduced imports, and these quotas were not lifted until the shipping shortage had become so acute as to make imports impossible in any case. Consequently, there were many shortages of imported foodstuffs by 1942, but in Surinam, which is self-sustaining, the shortage has proved to be more of an inconvenience to Europeans than a threat to the health of the population.

The agriculture of Surinam, however, has suffered from the loss of its European markets and markets in the United States could not be developed because of the curtailment of shipping space. The production of bauxite also has been limited by the available shipping rather than by the capacities of the plants.

The problems of agricultural labor in Surinam have been greatly aggravated by the high wages paid by the bauxite companies and by the deliberate policy pursued by the United States Army of raising wages beyond the possibility of competition. This expedient perhaps is justified by the necessity of building new roads, airports, and camp installations without delay, but it will result in future difficulties, as most laborers will be unwilling to return to the plantations at their former wages or at wages that are economically possible.

It is often said that wages in the West Indies are too low, and that the army has done only what should have been done before. But it is necessary to point out that the wage scale in the West Indies is already so high as to make competition with the Asiatic countries impossible in Europe and America, in spite of the fact that the former is much closer to these markets.

One result of the war has been the shifting of the principal offices of many important corporations from the Netherlands and the Netherlands East Indies to Willemstad and Paramaribo, and although these offices will eventually be returned to their former locations, this temporary shifting of the center of control will undoubtedly result in a better understanding of the problems of the West Indies Territories.

The war will effect certain long-range results that can be predicted with some accuracy at this time. A transference of trade from Europe to the United States occurred in the first World War, and although trade with Europe was resumed after the war, a larger percentage than before remained in the Western Hemisphere. This time the swing toward the United States has been far greater and it will be more lasting. New markets also have been opened in Argentina and Brazil that did not previously exist. In 1941 eighty per cent of Surinam's imports were from the United States, and more than ninety-three per cent of its exports were to the United States.

One of the stipulations of the peace is almost certain to be a policy of free trade in all dependent countries. There also is some reason to believe that after the war business will be conducted on a hemisphere basis. China, and probably Japan as well, will have to be given access to the raw materials of the East Indies and Malaya, and the East Indies is also the natural source of raw materials for Australia and New Zealand.

More sources of raw materials will have to be tapped in an increasingly industrialized world, and the development of the oriental countries with a concomitant increase in living standards will tend to lessen the present disparity of wages between the Orient and the Occident, and because of smaller shipping costs, will make it possible for Surinam's agricultural products to compete more favorably in the American and the European markets.

During the present war Surinam, in particular, has enjoyed greater contact with the outside world than has been the case for many years, and new ideas have been brought in by American troops that will affect the outlook of the people and even their customs. Curaçao, long a crossroads, will also be affected, for the concentration of troops there is much greater, and there will be a correspondingly greater knowledge of the Dutch territories in the United States.

The rise of air power has doubled the significance of the West Indian islands not only as defenses for the Panama Canal but also as stepping stones to the South American continent, an importance which cannot be overemphasized, and the establishment of American air bases on the British and Dutch islands makes it clear that the Caribbean area is coming more and more under the influence of the United States.

14

Netherlands America and the Future

Wʜᴀᴛ is to be the future of colonies, territories, and dominions after this war, which is being fought in the name of freedom for the common man? Is conquest to be the determining fact of whether a nation will become autonomous, or will there be a general reconsideration of the entire colonial problem, regardless of whether the status of the dependency has been affected by the war or not?

Mr. Sumner Welles voiced a widely held point of view when he said, "The war must assure the sovereign equality of people throughout the world. The age of imperialism is dead."

I do not quarrel with Mr. Welles' words, but with the interpretation that is likely to be placed upon them. If he is using the word "imperialism" as a synonym for "exploitation," there is no room for further argument, but if he means enlightened imperialism, or government in the best interests of the colonies, I find myself disagreeing with him.

The Caribbean peoples among others are not a homogeneous race. The Amerindian population is all but extinct, and in the Dutch territories the last remnants have been absorbed into the white and Negro populations. The Europeans, who came to the Caribbean in the past by the hundreds of thousands, today form only a transient and numerically small part of the population. The few permanent white settlers are economically and politically insignificant. The white man has been unable to compete with the Negro at physical labor, and his position has become largely executive or clerical.

Oriental laborers form so small a part of the Caribbean population as a whole that they need not be considered separately, except in the case of Surinam, British Guiana, and Trinidad. The Negroes, on the other hand, because of their great numerical superiority, their length of residence, and their adaptability to the climate, are gradually evolving into a new race, in which both African and European elements are fused.

The Amerindian has contributed a few words to Caribbean dialects and a few superstitions to Caribbean folklore, but very little else. Superficially, at least, Caribbean culture is almost wholly European. The religion, art, music, and language of Europe have been superimposed upon African emotional concepts that have been sublimated. In some islands the African influence is far stronger than in others but nowhere has it entirely disappeared.

The majority of the Caribbean islands are colonies of European or American powers. There are also a few republics, but even the worst of the colonies are better governed than the republics, which have been subject to revolution and every type of internal disorder. They have been in almost continuous financial difficulties, the instability of their governments has destroyed their trade, and their insignificance has left them helpless in world affairs.

All the Caribbean islands are either economically dependent or are in a very backward stage of development, judged by world standards.

The hypothesis of autonomy for all people is a romantic one, but one which can very easily be proved to be unworkable at

the present time. Most of the Caribbean islands are not economically independent, and many are not large enough ever to become so. Their small size limits the variety of their products and
consequently their industries. They cannot compete in a world
trade regulated by tariffs, and if it is argued that after the war
tariffs will be abolished—a very doubtful supposition—they cannot compete against large-scale machine agriculture to which in
most cases they are not suited. Furthermore, technological ad-
vances during the war and after it will result in the displace-
ment of many tropical products by substitutes, which will have
a profound effect on all tropical countries. What has in the past
happened to sugar, indigo, and dyewood may happen in the future to rubber, quinine, aluminum, and oil. Adjustments cannot
be made by small autonomous states with limited natural resources, and without sufficient capital to bridge the gap; it
would be impossible to interest outside capital under such spec-
ulative conditions.

One of the chief arguments for independence is that disin-
terest on the part of the home government may result in neglect
or that all trade may be directed to the mother country, even
though business might more profitably be conducted elsewhere.
It has also been argued that one colony may be enriched at the
expense of another. But these arguments are more than offset by
the fact that, without the backing of a strong central government, most of the colonies could not have been developed in the
first place, nor could they exist today. It is quite natural that
one colony may be more profitable than another and that the
profitable one will receive the most attention. It is equally true
that most Carribbean colonies have been operating at a deficit,
and since this deficit has been met by the parent country, the
colonies are better off than they would have been had they been
independent.

Politically, the argument against autonomy is even more

cogent. Self-government in the various Caribbean republics has already been demonstrated to be a failure, after many years of trial and error and in spite of much outside help, and there is no reason to believe that it would be any more successful in the islands which are now colonies, for they can not afford the complex machinery of government or of war.

The saying "Better freedom and a poor government than bondage and a good one" is one of those catch phrases so often used to arouse emotion and to obscure the truth. The world of the airplane and radio has became too small for the individual person or the individual country to act without respect for others. Furthermore, no small country can exist today unless its freedom is guaranteed by its more powerful neighbors, and freedom that can be given can also be withdrawn.

It has been my personal experience in the Caribbean countries and in the East that, although there is always a great deal of discussion about freedom and autonomy, the people who are the most vocal in their own behalf are the very ones who already enjoy a large measure of freedom, and they usually represent only a small fraction of the population. Many of them are politicians who hope to gain something by a change. Others have had a small amount of education, which has given them an urge to rule. Most of their thinking is destructive rather than constructive. They can find a hundred things wrong with their present situation, but could not devise a better system if their lives depended upon it.

To the majority of the population freedom means the ability to do what they want, and it does not make the slightest bit of difference whether the government is Dutch, English, or local, so long as it is equitable. But there are many native peoples who have learned that there is more true democracy in enlightened colonial government than there is in government by their own politicians. This is not an opinion. It is a fact which anyone can verify for himself by talking to the people—not to the politicians.

There is, of course, the possibility of a federation of Caribbean states, but the objections to this are similar to the objections against small individual states. Economically, a Caribbean federation, even if practical in other ways, would be better off only by comparison to a single state. The economy of the various islands is not complementary. Competition would still be severe, capital would still be lacking, and the entire alliance would still be dependent upon other countries for manufactured goods in exchange for agricultural products of very uncertain value.

The advocates of local autonomy cannot have rightly understood the historical lesson pointing to the increased importance of the Caribbean area to the United States. No nation, no matter how idealistic, can afford to leave itself open to attack, which means that whether these islands are governed locally, as a federation, or as the colonies of European countries, they can exist only because they are friendly to the United States. Expediency in this case *must* be the deciding factor.

Since the promulgation of the Monroe Doctrine, the tendency has been for the United States more and more to control Caribbean affairs. Geography shows the logic of this. In the past hundred years the United States has sent Marines into several Caribbean islands and Central American countries, has purchased the Danish Virgin Islands, held a protectorate over Cuba, and annexed Puerto Rico from Spain. More recently it has acquired naval and air bases from the British and has sent troops to help protect the Netherlands territories. Protection of the Panama Canal is today of paramount importance, and the rise of air power will make the Caribbean islands a vital link in our southern defenses.

At various times suggestions have been put forward, both in the United States and in Europe, that the United States buy the European colonies, or that they be transferred in payment of war debts. It is pointed out that many of these colonies are worthless to their owners, whereas they would at least be of strategic importance to the United States. Even without considering the matter of prestige involved, there are a number of reasons why this would not be as practical as it sounds. The Congress of the United States has been notoriously slow in accepting new territory, even when it was the express desire of the population of the territory, and there has been no indication in this instance that such is the case. There would probably also be considerable opposition from American labor unions, who would sense competition from labor, which, though expensive compared with the East, would still be cheap when contrasted to that of the United States.

Insofar as the Netherlands territories are concerned, the suggestion has already been countered in official circles by the statement that, according to the Netherlands Constitution, the Kingdom consists of territories in Europe, Asia, and America, with the Dutch East Indies, Surinam, and Curaçao ranking equally, and that no part can claim to possess any other part, much less the right to sell it.

If a change is to be made, it would best be accomplished gradually, and the European nations with colonies in the Caribbean already have had three hundred years of experience in colonial government and are best fitted to bring it about.

The problem has other ramifications. A very large percentage of the capital invested in the Caribbean countries is either European, or from the United States, and autonomy for all colonies throughout the world would mean nothing less than the complete dislocation of the economic life of countries with large colonial possessions. Surely this would not be a wise solution. On the other hand, if autonomy simply means freedom from European ties but a continuance of minority rule, there is nothing to gain and everything to lose.

Turning from the Caribbean as a whole to a consideration of the Dutch territories, I will anticipate the question: "What have the Dutch done during a period of three hundred years that they deserve to continue to rule these people?"

After studying these islands, the wonder grows that, with so little to work with, they should ever have figured in history at all, and one is forced to the conclusion that it was only the genius and persistence of the Dutch merchants and colonists that made this possible, when so many other Caribbean islands, so much more richly endowed by nature, remained in comparative obscurity. That more was not accomplished was due in part to the times.

Warfare was endemic in the Caribbean for centuries, and international rivalry often destroyed in a day what had been built up over many painful years. Furthermore, it is not possible to judge earlier colonial policy by present-day standards. Hindsight is always better than foresight.

Colonial policy has had its dark side, but there is no question that its evolution has been continually toward humanity and justice to the people governed. In short, it has kept pace with the morality of the times.

Colonial administration is not learned overnight and involves more than a knowledge of language and primitive law. Its basis is a deep interest in the races governed.

The Dutch have neither the aloof attitude of the British nor the careless attitude of the French. Their liberal treatment of native races is a result of many years of experience, but they have had the good sense not to attempt to educate natives to European standards in one or two generations, and the equal good sense to educate themselves in the philosophy and psychology of these peoples.

Knowledge is worth more than any amount of good will and idealism.

Two Councils recently have been created to bring the Governments of the four Territories of the Netherlands Kingdom closer together and to give wider representation to the three Overseas Territories. They are the Buitengewone Raad van Advies, which will advise the central government in London during the war, and the Rijkconferentie or Imperiale Raad, which will meet after the war to draw up new reforms.

The basic idea is a Kingdom of the Netherlands which will have four more or less equal parts. The exact details are yet to be worked out by the Council, but it is likely that each part will be represented according to its importance, perhaps in a similar manner to the representation of our states in Congress. This will not be easy as there are many factors involved, but some indication of the solution can be given by considering the size of the Territories, their population, and the number of their representatives at the Rijkconferentie:

TERRITORY	AREA	POPULATION	REPRESENT-ATIVES
Netherlands in Europe	13,604	8,800,000	15
Netherlands East Indies	735,267	72,000,000	15
Surinam	55,143	183,730	3
Territory of Curaçao	384	119,585	3

This development is in the true spirit of international thought, which must be the key to the future. It allows the widest possible development of each individual Territory in its own interest as well as for the good of the whole. The trend of the times is away from the small concepts of nationalism raised by racial differences and the accidents of geography. Modern methods of transportation and radio have brought the peoples of the world together in time and space and have created common interests which previously did not exist, but local autonomy for each small group of people would be a reversion to the worst type of nationalism. Probably the future lies in a World State or a World Federation. If it is suggested that colonies be granted local autonomy under a mandate or protectorate, the answer is obvious: mandate and protectorate should be synonyms for enlightened imperialism.

Mutual knowledge and understanding of other nations, not the raising of any more artificial barriers, is the basis for future peace.

It appears likely that the *status quo ante* will be maintained immediately following the war and that any changes will be gradual. The Netherlands West Indies probably will not see any fighting, therefore, it will not have to dig itself out of the ruins nor will it have been subject to starvation and brutalization. In these respects it will have the advantage over the East Indies. It will not be the subject of peace negotiations and will not have to suffer interim government by the army or navy, consequently it will be able to proceed immediately in reconstructing its agriculture and trade. In this it will be hampered only by the fact that the Government of the Netherlands will be in a state of considerable confusion with many more important matters to be settled. The Netherlands West Indies will have to look out for itself, but, with the promise of a large measure of self-government, it should gladly shoulder the responsibility.

Appendixes

APPENDIX I

AREAS OF THE NETHERLANDS WEST INDIES*
(*In Square Miles*)

Territory of Curaçao

Curaçao	172.5†
Aruba	69.9
Bonaire	111.9‡
St. Martin	13.2
Saba	4.8
St. Eustatius	11.8
TOTAL	384.1

Surinam

55,143.0

Netherlands West Indies

55,527.1

* Official figures of the Curaçao and Surinam Governments.
† Includes Klein Curaçao.
‡ Includes Klein Bonaire.

APPENDIX II

POPULATION OF THE NETHERLANDS WEST INDIES

*Territory of Curaçao**

Curaçao	73,343	
Aruba	35,933	
Bonaire	5,725	
St. Martin	2,337	
Saba	1,229	
St. Eustatius	1,018	
TOTAL		119,585

Surinam†

Paramaribo District	56,233	
Surinam District	46,377	
Saramacca District	9,866	
Commewijne District	25,963	
Coronie District	4,278	
Nickerie District	15,650	
Marowijne District	3,715	
Bush Negroes and Indians Scattered Among the Above Districts	21,648	
TOTAL		183,730

Netherlands West Indies

303,315

* Official figures of the Curaçao Government as of July 1, 1943.
† Official figures of the Surinam Government as of December 31, 1941.

APPENDIX III

POPULATION ACCORDING TO RACES

Territory of Curaçao*	Curaçao	Aruba	Bonaire	St. Martin	Saba	St. Eustatius	Total
Netherlands citizens born in							
Territory of Curaçao	57,413	23,344	5,509	1,676	1,194	915	90,051
Netherlands	4,436	645	51	16	3	5	5,156
Netherlands East Indies	385	29	10	—	7	—	424
Surinam	2,523	985	16	5	7	5	3,541
Elsewhere	1,728	1,002	43	227	13	—	3,013
Sub-total	66,485	26,005	5,629	1,924	1,217	925	102,185
Venezuelans	2,234	1,961	16	2	—	—	4,213
Portuguese	222	18	—	—	—	—	240
Americans	117	1,772	1	8	11	7	1,916
English	2,761	4,377	2	289	—	82	7,511
Dominicans	175	676	1	7	—	4	863
Colombians	185	222	—	—	—	—	407
Syrians	171	30	13	—	—	—	214
Poles	71	55	—	—	—	—	126
Roumanians	115	10	—	—	—	—	125
Chinese	500	—	—	—	—	—	500
Other nationalities	835	917	63	106	1	—	1,922
Without nationality	72	21	—	1	—	—	94
Sub-total	6,958	10,059	96	413	12	93	18,131
TOTAL	73,943	36,064	5,725	2,337	1,229	1,018	120,316

* Official figures of the Curaçao Government for July 1, 1943.

APPENDIX III

POPULATION ACCORDING TO RACES
(*Continued*)

Surinam*

Europeans born in the Netherlands	1,015
Europeans born elsewhere	1,043
Negroes and Mulattoes	70,415
British Indians	49,300
Indonesians—primarily Javanese	34,563
Chinese	2,298
Others	3,448
Sub-total	162,082
Bush Negroes	19,032
Aboriginal Indians	2,616
Sub-total	21,648
TOTAL	183,730

* Official figures of the Surinam Government for December 31, 1941.

APPENDIX IV

POPULATION ACCORDING TO RELIGIONS

Territory of Curaçao*	Curaçao	Aruba	Bonaire	St. Martin	Saba	St. Eustatius	Total
United Protestant	3,364	3,271	90	4	—	—	6,729
Netherlands Reformed	2,187	405	13	—	—	—	2,605
Reformed	264	43	—	—	—	—	307
Roman Catholic	61,612	27,510	5,566	700	780	358	96,526
Jews	735	189	4	—	—	—	928
Methodist	1,352	2,284	—	1,631	4	540	5,811
Anglican	1,024	1,578	—	—	428	—	3,030
Seventh Day Adventist	55	15	2	—	—	120	192
Confucianists	500	—	—	—	—	—	500
Other religions†	1,276	479	14	2	17	—	1,788
No religion or religion unknown	1,470	290	36	—	—	—	1,796
TOTAL	73,839	36,064	5,725	2,337	1,229	1,018	120,212

* Official figures of the Curaçao Government for July 1, 1943.
† Includes Baptist, Pilgrim Holiness, and Evangelical Lutheran churches.

APPENDIX IV

POPULATION ACCORDING TO RELIGIONS
(*Continued*)

Surinam

Netherlands Reformed		8,875*
Evangelical Lutheran	Europeans	3,945*
Moravian	and	30,870*
Roman Catholic	Natives	30,240*
Jews		800*
Mohammedans	British Indians and Indonesians	45,300*
Hindus	British Indians	36,100*
Confucianists	Chinese	1,390*
Others†	Various	4,562*
Sub-total		162,082
Animists	Bush Negroes and Aboriginal Indians	21,648‡
TOTAL		183,730

* These figures are estimates computed by the author and are based on figures for 1937 published in the *Surinam Report 1938* with compensations for population increases.

‡ Total Bush Negro and Aboriginal Indian population figures are given though Moravian missionaries have converted a few Bush Negroes and Catholic missionaries a few Aboriginal Indians.

† Includes Evangelic, Mennonite, and African Methodist Episcopal churches.

APPENDIX V

POPULATION TRENDS IN THE NETHERLANDS WEST INDIES

Curaçao		*Aruba*		*Bonaire*	
1635	1,447	1816	1,732	1816	1,135
1815	12,840	1860	2,849	1849	2,159
1859	32,200	1870	3,726	1865	3,579
1865	19,864	1888	7,365	1896	4,529
1891	26,584	1900	9,702	1912	6,427
1912	32,926	1912	9,441	1943	5,725
1943	73,343	1943	35,933		

Saba		St. Martin	
1665	226	1770	4,157
1870	1,832	1816	3,595
1890	1,883	1860	3,157
1914	1,449	1865	2,853
1943	1,229	1890	3,882
		1914	3,309
		1943	2,337

St. Eustatius		Surinam†	
1665	1,600	1738	52,827
1718	20,000*	1785	55,000
1786	7,600	1805	64,602
1815	2,591	1831	61,511
1860	1,927	1863	52,963
1865	1,890	1900	67,968
1890	1,588	1914	85,536
1914	1,437	1942	183,730
1943	1,018		

* The *Encyclopedie van Nederlandsch West-Indië* estimates the population of St. Eustatius in 1718 as 20,000 to 25,000 but concludes that this figure is unreliable.

† Figures 1738-1914 do not include Bush Negroes or Aboriginal Indians, whereas the 1942 figure includes 21,648 Bush Negroes and Aboriginal Indians.

APPENDIX VI

VITAL STATISTICS FOR THE NETHERLANDS WEST INDIES FOR THE YEAR 1941*

Territory of Curaçao

	Births	Per Thousand	Deaths	Per Thousand
Curaçao	1,925	28.2	746	10.9
Aruba	1,163	36.9	172	5.5
Bonaire	135	24.3	85	15.2
St. Martin	69	35.6	38	19.6
Saba	35	30.5	16	13.9
St. Eustatius	35	28.8	16	13.1
TOTAL	3,362	30.7	1,973	9.8

Surinam

	Births	Per Thousand	Deaths	Per Thousand
	5,140	31.7	1,928	11.9

* Official figures of the Curaçao and Surinam Governments.

The extremely low death rate on Aruba is not unusual and is due to the fact that young, strong men come to work in the refineries, also to the excellent medical attention.

The higher death rates of Bonaire, St. Martin, Saba, and St. Eustatius are due to the fact that many of the younger men and women have left these islands to work in Curaçao and Aruba and because medical facilities are limited.

APPENDIX VII

TEMPERATURE AND RAINFALL OF THE NETHERLANDS WEST INDIES

TEMPERATURE*
(In Degrees Fahrenheit)

Mean Temperature	Willemstad Curaçao 1910-1942	Philipsburg St. Martin 1920-1942	Paramaribo Surinam 1899-1940
Annual	81.4	80.4	79.3
Warmest Month	83.3 (Sept.)	82.2 (Aug.-Sept.)	80.9 (Sept.)
Coolest Month	78.4 (Jan.)	76.5 (Jan.-Feb.)	77.5 (Jan.)

* Variations in temperature between day and night are greater than the annual range in Willemstad, Philipsburg, and Paramaribo.

RAINFALL†
(In Inches)

Mean Rainfall	1894-1942	1892-1942	1847-1940
Annual	22.5	42.9	90.5
Rainiest Month	5.0 (Nov.)	5.8 (Nov.)	12.2 (May)
Driest Month	0.5 (May)	1.6 (Mar.)	3.0 (Oct.)

† Curaçao, Leeward and Windward Islands: The rainy season is considered to be from October to December, but this season is not always well defined.

Surinam: There are two rainy seasons and two dry seasons as follows: small rainy season, December to February; small dry season, March to April; big rainy season, May to July; and big dry season, August to November.

Temperature and rainfall figures have been computed from tables in *The European Possessions in the Caribbean Area*, American Geographical Society, Map of Hispanic American Publication No. 4, 1941, based on *Het Klimaat van Nederlandsch West-Indië*, C. Brack, Koninklijk Nederlandsch Meteorologisch Instituut, No. 102, Mededeelingen en Verhandelingen 36, The Hague, 1935; on *Surinam—A Geographic Study*, J. Warren Nystrom, The Netherlands Information Bureau, 1942; and from figures direct from the Surinam and Curaçao Governments.

Curaçao figures represent an average of nineteen stations.

The rainfall of Curaçao and Bonaire is about equal, but Aruba is somewhat drier. Precipitation in Saba is greater than in St. Martin, and in St. Eustatius less than in St. Martin.

APPENDIX VIII

BUDGETS FOR THE NETHERLANDS
WEST INDIES, 1938-42*
(*In Guilders*)

Territory of Curaçao

Year	Revenues	Expenditures	Balance
1938	10,758,605	10,001,153	757,452
1939	13,404,693	12,811,342	593,351
1940	11,249,660	12,118,652	*868,992*
1941	14,219,665	13,034,000†	1,185,665
1942	19,969,917	19,136,525‡	833,392‡

Surinam

Year	Revenues	Expenditures	Balance
1938	4,247,882	6,760,223	*2,512,341*
1939	4,551,419	7,466,922	*2,915,503*
1940	4,742,692	6,720,746	*1,978,054*
1941	6,928,644	6,927,552	1,090
1942	8,643,417‡	8,628,515‡	14,902‡

Figures in italics represent deficits.

* Official figures of the Curaçao and Surinam Governments.

† Includes Fl. 1,370,000 voluntary gift to the Empire for war work.

‡ Estimated.

APPENDIX IX

CHIEF SOURCES OF REVENUE OF THE NETHERLANDS WEST INDIES

(In 1,000 Guilders)

1928-1937

Territory of Curaçao

	1928	1929	1930	1931	1932	1933	1934	1935	1936	1937
Import Duty	1,525	2,152	2,111	455	1,275	1,507	1,673	1,917	2,070	2,425
Income Tax	337	914	1,048	1,514	1,787	1,138	2,388	1,911	1,701	1,763
Excise Duty on Liquor	1,065	1,119	1,271	1,000	641	694	797	840	873	946
Pilot Fees	664	793	770	632	618	794	805	792	873	920
Land Tax	111	357	421	416	491	538	472	463	561	487

Surinam

	1928	1929	1930	1931	1932	1933	1934	1935	1936	1937
Import Duty	1,843	1,790	1,792	1,580	1,421	1,326	1,330	1,329	1,365	1,433
Income Tax	484	461	447	484	368	286	313	284	283	414
School Fees	77	71*	150*	162*	163*	155*	152*	148*	148*	143
Tel. & Post Service	161	142	141	145	105	105	113	110	118	140
Rent Tax on Liquor Shops	104	127	115	86	112	104	103	107	106	123

* This amount includes a partial payment of school fees levied by the denominational education boards.

APPENDIX X

IMPORTS AND EXPORTS OF THE NETHERLANDS WEST INDIES
(*In Guilders*)

Territory of Curaçao

Year	Imports	Exports
1935	30,593,570	1,124,983
	143,571,231	*166,131,856*
1936	28,538,756	1,330,756
	168,473,620	*200,181,862*
1937	43,112,304	3,277,190
	254,174,005	*266,666,763*
1938	41,205,524	2,260,818
	138,740,326	*151,026,135*
1939	33,341,481	2,481,822
	116,536,346	**
1940	27,459,989	14,278,385*
	**	**
1941	42,170,381	9,373,311
	**	**
1942	67,354,984†	5,491,221
	**	**

Surinam

Year	Imports	Exports
1936	5,752,079	5,181,299
1937	6,866,542	7,613,210
1938	6,861,756	6,609,139
1939	7,882,353	7,959,210
1940	8,519,684	7,319,419
1941	9,429,922	11,398,377

Roman figures indicate imports and exports excluding petroleum products. Italics represent petroleum products.

* Of this figure Fl. 11,428,829 represents gold in bars exported to the United States.

** Figures for petroleum products are no longer given out.

† This figure reflects a rise in prices rather than an increase in imports.

Figures for 1935-7 are from *Curaçaosch Verslag 1938* and for 1938-40 from *Jaarverslag van de Kamer van Koophandel en Nijverheid, op Curaçao over het Jaar 1940*. Figures 1941-2 from the Curaçao Government.

Figures 1936-40 from *Suriname Handelsstatistiek 1940:* 1941 figure direct from the Surinam Government.

APPENDIX XI

TERRITORY OF CURAÇAO TRADE WITH THE MOST IMPORTANT COUNTRIES

(In Guilders)

IMPORTS

Countries	1937			1940
	Total	*Petroleum Products*	*Other than Petroleum Products*	*Other than Petroleum Products*
Netherlands	8,878,072	4,705	8,874,467	3,043,164
United States	37,631,805	16,746,705	20,885,100	16,138,502
Venezuela	223,885,759	223,039,201	846,588	650,766
Colombia	10,134,127	9,806,490	327,637	178,096
Mexico	3,600,976	3,591,354	9,622	3,588
Japan	2,924,249		2,924,249	1,634,106
Germany	2,609,573	9,183	2,600,390	66,539
England	2,355,324	15,200	2,340,124	2,030,685
English Antilles	921,964	803,751	118,213	27,022
France	562,796		562,796	221,765
Santo Domingo	512,187		512,187	640,954
Argentine	190,434		190,434	525,259
TOTAL IMPORTS	297,286,309	254,169,005	43,117,304	27,459,989

APPENDIX XI

TERRITORY OF CURAÇAO TRADE WITH THE MOST IMPORTANT COUNTRIES

(Continued)

EXPORTS

Countries	1937 Total	1937 Petroleum Products	1937 Other than Petroleum Products	1940 Other than Petroleum Products
Netherlands	27,503,650	26,983,892	519,758	54,874
United States	32,571,614	31,946,298	625,316	11,836,375*
England	88,537,718	88,362,357	175,361	11,024
Germany	14,724,659	14,554,198	170,461	———
French West Africa	11,444,323	11,390,271	54,052	
Argentine	9,855,642	9,853,369	2,273	1,882
Brazil	9,551,396	9,551,396	———	1,185
Italy	7,173,933	7,172,521	1,412	———
France	6,131,171	6,123,620	7,551	2,408
Sweden	5,706,750	5,656,248	50,502	4,439
French Antilles	48,255	10,126	38,129	604,553
Venezuela	1,546,373	1,384,113	162,260	255,543
TOTAL EXPORTS	269,943,953	266,666,763	3,277,190	14,278,385

* Of this figure Fl. 11,428,929 represents gold in bars.
1937 figures are from *Curaçaosch Verslag 1938*, and 1940 figures are from *Jaarverslag van de Kamer van Koophandel en Nijverheid 1940.*

APPENDIX XII

SURINAM

TRADE WITH THE MOST IMPORTANT COUNTRIES*
(In Percentages of the Total Value)

IMPORTS†

Countries	1928	1935	1938	1939	1940	1941
Netherlands	51.3	39.4	36.5	34.4	13.5	—
United States	29.8	18.8	26.0	30.0	57.5	71.9
Great Britain	1.2	12.3	7.3	5.3	6.3	4.2
France	0.9	0.9	0.7	0.7	0.7	0.3
Germany	0.8	4.6	4.4	4.4	0.4	—
British Guiana	12.8	1.2	0.7	0.2	0.4	0.2
Canada	—	2.0	1.1	1.1	2.3	3.6
Trinidad	1.7	3.8	3.6	4.8	3.4	5.4
Japan	—	8.4	8.7	9.4	7.0	3.4
Argentine	—	1.8	2.2	2.5	2.2	4.6
Brazil	—	—	0.3	0.2	1.1	1.3

EXPORTS†

Countries	1928	1935	1938	1939	1940	1941
Netherlands	57.6	44.0	26.3	16.5	1.5	—
United States	22.6	46.8	58.4	71.8	90.5	93.4
Great Britain	13.2	1.7	3.1	1.8	3.8	4.2
France	0.3	0.3	0.2	0.4	—	—
Germany	—	0.4	1.5	0.6	—	—
British Guiana	1.2	1.6	0.6	1.6	1.1	0.5
Martinique	—	—	2.2	1.3	0.1	—
Guadeloupe	—	—	3.1	2.8	0.5	—
Curaçao	1.1	0.4	0.7	1.0	0.9	1.8
Norway	0.1	3.9	2.3	1.6	0.8	—

* Official figures of the Surinam Government.

† Excluding gold and silver coins for the years 1940 and 1941, also arms and munitions for the year 1941.

APPENDIX XIII

SURINAM

EXPORTS OF THE MOST IMPORTANT PRODUCTS*

(*In Quantities*)

Product	Unit	1928	1935	1938	1939	1940	1941
Mineral							
Bauxite	Met. Ton	206,767	115,189	377,598	504,062	615,534	1,093,764
			1,439,865	*3,826,492*	*5,293,747*	*6,353,632*	
Gold	Gram	145,798	398,095	485,181	344,820	**	**
			557,332	*839,364*	*606,882*	**	**
Agricultural							
Sugar	Kg.	15,621,794	15,065,071	10,920,310	8,282,814	6,404,200	9,389,600
			482,083	*546,016*	*410,353*	*319,353*	
Coffee	Kg.	3,455,917	4,479,886	2,784,905	2,487,067	626,661	1,065,785
			898,480	*465,920*	*592,786*	*141,957*	
Rice	Kg.	727,317	4,555	7,401,472	6,494,997	1,536,571	1,520,500
			285	*441,898*	*380,813*	*115,194*	
Oranges	Pc.	374,408	422,677	646,332	668,052	142,458	278,469
			5,156	*8,770*	*9,611*	*2,369*	
Molasses	Liter	—	3,584,393	3,418,767	2,498,688	2,877,642	4,074,946
			19,914	*34,188*	*24,986*	*28,777*	
Rum	Liter	362,112	126,114	157,699	162,860	130,894	128,110
			11,350	*16,246*	*18,322*	*17,382*	
Balata	Kg.	520,484	143,524	277,338	370,907	192,698	275,097
			135,778	*312,770*	*437,062*	*277,389*	
Corn	Kg.	67,240	5,840	120,215	35,592	6,325	326,350

* Official figures of the Surinam Government.
** Figures for the import and export of gold are no longer given out.
Figures in italics represent values in guilders.

APPENDIX XIV

COMPARISON OF THE MOST IMPORTANT EXPORTS FOR THE TERRITORY OF CURAÇAO AND SURINAM FOR 1937

(In Guilders)

Territory of Curaçao		*Surinam*	
Petroleum Products	266,666,763	Bauxite	4,904,116
Phosphate of Lime	873,404	Gold	743,765
Goat Skins	207,247	Sugar	621,992
Aloes	111,433	Coffee	529,416
Divi-divi Pods	32,413	Rice	413,992
Irish Potatoes	5,341	Balata	189,750
Sweet Potatoes	3,128	Molasses	32,109
Cattle	2,549	Rum	28,182
Total exports excluding petroleum products	3,277,190*	Total exports excluding bauxite	2,709,094

Curaçao figures are from *Curaçaosch Verslag 1938*: Surinam figures from *Suriname Handelsstatistiek 1940*. 1937 was selected for this comparison as it was a normal year unaffected by war.
* Includes some items previously imported.

APPENDIX XV

ANALYSIS OF TRENDS IN THE PETROLEUM INDUSTRY OF CURAÇAO AND ARUBA

(Amounts in 1,000 Barrels)

Imports of Crude Petroleum

Year	Venezuela	Colombia
1937	141,455	6,027
1938	149,825	9,066

Crude Petroleum Refined—by Companies

Year	C.P.I.M.	Arend	Lago	Total
1925	9,354	—	—	9,354
1930	50,575	7,193	34,819*	92,587
1935	45,224	2,830	59,459	107,513
1936	47,555	2,190	68,442*	118,187
1937	56,946*	—	82,673	—

Petroleum Products Exported

Year	Amount	Year	Amount
1918	40	1930	102,318
1920	635	1932	89,822
1921	1,213	1934	104,408
1927	27,533	1937	145,376
1928	71,898	1938	165,046

Petroleum Products Exported to the Most Important Countries

Year	To the United States	To the Netherlands	To Great Britain
1929	42,052	1,580	6,884
1935	21,371	3,701	29,787
1937	26,851	11,702	35,089
1938*	27,894	15,849	37,938

Gasoline Only

Year	To the United States	To the Netherlands	To Great Britain
1929	7,157	—	2,257
1935	98	2,911	13,424
1937	205	2,663	15,318
1938	3	3,345	16,817

Fuel Oil Only

Year	To the United States	To the Netherlands	To Great Britain
1929	21,897	73	9,486
1935	18,618	1,194	9,268
1937	23,758	2,637	13,866
1938	24,563	4,549	13,942

* Net imports of crude petroleum.

All figures are from A. H. Redfield, *The Petroleum Trade of the Netherlands West Indies*, Bureau of Mines, United States Department of the Interior.

In 1938, 45.1 per cent of the petroleum products used by Germany came from the Netherlands West Indies and Venezuela.

APPENDIX XVI
AMOUNT AND VALUE OF PHOSPHATE EXPORTS OF MIJNMAATSCHAPPIJ CURAÇAO
1935-41

Year	Metric Tons	Value in Guilders
1935	90,709	702,758
1936	78,131	600,818
1937	101,837	873,404
1938	99,283	888,723
1939*	64,072	501,825
1940*	6,047	53,010
1941	+ 100,000	**

Figures for 1935-7 are from *Curaçaosch Verslag 1938;* 1938-40 from *Jaarverslag van de Kamer van Koophandel en Nijverheid op Curaçao over het Jaar 1940:* 1941 figure estimated by Mr. A. Leaver, Director of Mijnmaatschappij Curaçao.

* The years 1939-40 mark a period of transition. Prior to the war phosphate was exported to the Netherlands, Germany, and the Scandinavian countries: today almost all phosphate goes to England.

** Figures are no longer given out.

APPENDIX XVII
SHIPPING IN THE NETHERLANDS WEST INDIES
Curaçao*

Year	Steamships	Net Cap. in M³	Sailing Ships	Net Cap. in M³
1933	4,824	28,680,985	1,232	97,698
1934	4,877	28,862,237	1,336	108,207
1935	5,047	29,662,634	1,574	158,400
1936	5,241	31,070,808	1,876	154,383
1937	5,657	33,619,960	1,822	152,137
1938	6,872	41,635,399	1,766	168,394
1939	6,140	37,166,137	1,565	173,043

Surinam†

Year	Steamships	Net Reg. Tons	Sailing Ships	Net Reg. Tons
1934	205	283,394	25	1,431
1935	197	296,347	30	759
1936	262	357,979	23	770
1937	392	487,996	17	1,222
1938	423	488,895	12	766
1939	432	515,418	17	550

* Figures are from *Jaaverslag van de Kamer van Koophandel en Niverheid, over het Jaar 1936 en 1939.*

† Figures are from the *Statistical Annual of Surinam.*

APPENDIX XVIII

SCHOOL SYSTEM OF THE NETHERLANDS WEST INDIES*

Territory of Curaçao

NUMBER OF PUPILS

	No. of Schools	No. of Teachers	Government Schools	Roman Catholic Schools	Other Private Schools	Expenses from Public Treasury
Curaçao	28	165	674	7,475	582	Fl. 570,366.41
Aruba	11	43	228	2,434	283	138,846.49
Bonaire	3	16	—	883	—	41,115.53
St. Martin	5	17	278	242	—	48,835.15
Saba	4	7	48	133	—	17,547.00
St. Eustatius	2	4	112	85	—	10,599.00
TOTAL	53	252	1,340	11,252	865	Fl. 827,309.58

Surinam

Number of Schools	122
Number of Teachers	470
Number of Pupils:	
Government Schools	7,478
Non-aided Denominational Schools	284
Roman Catholic Schools	7,405
Moravian Schools	5,340
Baptist Schools	817
African Methodist Episcopal Schools	527
TOTAL	21,851

Grants in aid to Denominational Schools:
Fl. 692,343.40

*Figures as of January 1, 1938.

APPENDIX XIX

LIVESTOCK IN THE NETHERLANDS WEST INDIES

1937

Territory of Curaçao

	Horses	Donkeys	Mules	Cattle	Goats	Sheep	Pigs	Carabao
Curaçao	56	2,231	21	1,604	23,401	7,628	1,626	—
Aruba	5	845	—	915	11,080	14,150	1,023	—
Bonaire	52	1,000	2	20	30,000	11,000	440	—
St. Martin	63	88	—	1,249	1,196	1,157	335	—
St. Eustatius	41	417	1	815	887	1,286	321	—
Saba	12	60	—	162	529	274	209	—
TOTAL	229	4,641	24	4,765	67,093	35,495	3,954	—

Surinam

	Horses	Donkeys	Mules	Cattle	Goats	Sheep	Pigs	Carabao
Surinam	474	1,165	120	21,209	4,912	729	7,109	48

Netherlands West Indies

	Horses	Donkeys	Mules	Cattle	Goats	Sheep	Pigs	Carabao
Netherlands West Indies	703	5,806	144	25,974	72,005	36,224	11,063	48

APPENDIX XX

[SLAVES EMANCIPATED IN THE NETHERLANDS WEST INDIES AND INDEMNITIES PAID

Territory of Curaçao

	Total Slaves	Government Slaves	Against Indemnity	Indemnity Per Slave	Total Indemnity
Curaçao	6,751	67	6,684	Fl. 200	Fl. 1,336,800
Aruba	480	6	474	200	94,800
Bonaire	758	607	151	200	30,200
St. Martin	1,878	—	1,878	100*	187,800
Saba	700	—	700	200	140,000
St. Eustatius	1,087	—	1,087	200	217,400
Sub-Total	*11,654*	*680*	*10,974*	—	*2,007,000*

Surinam

	Total Slaves	Government Slaves	Against Indemnity	Indemnity Per Slave	Total Indemnity
	33,621	*649*	*32,972*	*300*	*9,891,600*
TOTAL	45,275	1,329	43,946	—	11,898,600

Emancipation took place on July 1, 1863.

* The original indemnity per slave for St. Martin was Fl. 30, but this was increased by the law of July 5, 1864, to Fl. 100.

APPENDIX XXI

ROYAL DUTCH AIR LINES—KONINKLIJKE LUCHTVAART MAATSCHAPPIJ

Extension of Services by Years

1935	Curaçao—Aruba
1936	Curaçao—Aruba—Maracaibo
1937	Curaçao—La Guaira
1938	Curaçao—Coro
1939	Curaçao—Aruba—Maracaibo—Barranquilla
	Curaçao—La Guaira—Trinidad—Paramaribo
	Trinidad—Barbados (since discontinued)
1940	Trinidad—Ciudad Bolivar (since discontinued)
1941	Curaçao—Aruba—Jamaica
1942-3	Curaçao—Aruba—Jamaica/Haiti—Havana—Miami

Total length of lines increased from 125 kilometers on December 31, 1935 to 4,119 kilometers on December 31, 1941. Transatlantic service between the Netherlands, Curaçao, and Surinam, which was about to begin when hostilities broke out, has been postponed until after the war.

	Revenue Passenger/Kms Sold	Revenue Passengers Carried	Excess Baggage Carried Kgs	Air Express Carried Kgs	Air Mail Carried Kgs	Kilometers Flown	Hours Flown
1935	Figures Not Available	2,645	4,418	3,991	307	65,460	406
1941	5,490,116	20,513	133,487	64,614	13,854	962,036	3,936
First Six Months 1942	4,599,044	11,496	40,765	56,635	8,387	683,528	2,505
Total 1935 to June 30, 1942	Figures Not Available	86,458	446,964	279,401	55,975	4,419,057	18,618

In comparison with the first year (1935) of operations in the West Indies, the year 1941 and the first six months of 1942 showed very marked increases.

It is interesting to note that not a single personal accident occurred during the 4,419,057 kilometers flown in seven and a half years of operation.

July 1942 shows an all-time high of 2,365 passengers carried.

Services are now being carried on with the original three-engined Fokker F-18 flown from the Netherlands in 1934 and by four Lockheeds delivered in 1938. Two Douglas DC-5s delivered in 1940 were subsequently transferred to the Netherlands East Indies.

Bibliography

BOOKS

ALTING, J. H. CARPENTIER & BUNING, W. DE COCK. The Netherlands and the World War. Studies in the war history of a neutral. Vol. III. The effect of the war upon the colonies. Published for the Carnegie Endowment for International Peace. Economic and social history of the world war. New Haven: Yale University Press, 1928. 135 p.

ANGELINO, A. D. A. DE KAT. Colonial policy. Abridged translation from the Dutch by G. J. Renier, in collaboration with the author. Chicago: The University of Chicago Press, 1931. 2 v.

The Aruba Gold Mining Company, Limited. Registered July 4th, 1872. Nominal capital, £500,000 in 50,000 shares of £10 each. London: 1872. [A report.] 74 p., map.

BAKER, CECIL SHERMAN & THOMPSON, WALLACE. Climatic influences in the Caribbean. *Current History*, Vol. XXXI, No. 5, February 1930. p. 908-18, illus., map.

BALLOU, H. A. The Dutch Leeward Islands. *Tropical Agriculture*, the official journal of the Imperial College of Tropical Agriculture, Trinidad, B. W. I., Vol. XI, No. 12, December 1934. p. 317-20.

BARBOUR, VIOLET. Privateers and pirates of the West Indies. *American Historical Review*, Vol. XVI, No. 3, April 1911. p. 529-66, bibl.

BENJAMINS, DR. H. D. & SNELLEMAN, JNO. F. Encyclopaedie van Nederlandsch West-Indië. The Hague, 1914-17.

BRETT, REV. WILLIAM HENRY. The Indian tribes of Guiana; their condition and habits. With researches into their past history, superstitions, legends, antiquities, languages, &c. London: Bell and Daldy, 1868. 500 p., illus., map.

CLELAND, HERDMAN F. Curaçao, a losing colonial venture. *Bulletin of the American Geographical Society*, Vol. XLI, No. 3, 1909. p. 129-38, illus., map.

CUNDALL, FRANK. The migration from Surinam to Jamaica. *Timehri,* Vol. VI, Third Series, September 1919. p. 145-72.

DENTZ, FRED OUDSCHANS. Surinam as a Dutch possession. *Timehri,* Vol. VI, Third Series, September 1919. p. 173-82.

DESBRIERE, JUANITA. Aruba, Cinderella of the Caribbean.—Two fairy godmothers tried to bring fame to this little island through her mineral charms; but as a distributing center for "liquid gold," "Cinderella" finally came into her own. *Natural History,* Vol. XLI, No. 2, February 1938. p. 138-40, 148.

DUNBAR, ELIZABETH U. What oil did to Curaçao. *Journal of Geography,* Vol. XXXIII, No. 9, December 1934. p. 340-5, illus., maps, figs.

EDLER, FRIEDRICH. The Dutch republic and the American revolution. Johns Hopkins University studies in history and political science. Under the direction of the departments of history, political economy, and political science. Series XXIX, No. 2. Baltimore: The Johns Hopkins Press, 1911. 246 p., bibl.

Great Britain. Foreign Office, Historical Section. Dutch Guiana. Handbooks prepared under the direction of the Historical Section of the Foreign Office.—No. 136. *In* Peace handbooks, Vol. XXI, North, Central and South America: Atlantic Islands. London: Published by H. M. Stationery Office, 1920. 79 p., bibl.

HERSKOVITS, MELVILLE J. & HERSKOVITS, FRANCES S. Rebel destiny. Among the Bush-Negroes of Dutch Guiana. New York: Whittlesey House, 1934. 366 p., illus.

——— Suriname folk-lore. With transcriptions of Suriname songs and musical analysis by Dr. M. Kolinski. Part I.—Notes on the culture of the Paramaribo Negroes. Part II.—Stories, riddles, proverbs, and dreams. Part III.—Music. Columbia University contributions to Anthropology, Vol. XXVII. New York: Columbia University Press, 1936. 766 p., illus., bibl.

HISS, PHILIP HANSON. A selective guide to the English literature on the Netherlands West Indies. With a supplement on British Guiana. Booklets of the Netherlands Information Bureau, No. 9. New York: The Netherlands Information Bureau, 1943. xiv, 124 p.

HOUSTON, HILL. Surinam. *Foreign Commerce Weekly,* Vol. V, No. 6, November 8, 1941. p. 4-5, 36-7, illus.

HYNAM, C. A. S. Agriculture in the Dutch Windward Islands. *Tropical Agriculture,* the official journal of the Imperial College of Tropical Agriculture, Trinidad, B. W. I. Vol. XVIII, No. 7, July 1941. p. 135-8.

KAHN, MORTON C. Djuka. The Bush Negroes of Dutch Guiana. New York: The Viking Press, 1931. 233 p., illus., bibl.

KRUYTHOFF, S. J. The Netherlands Windward Islands and a few interesting items on French St. Martin. A handbook of useful information for visitor as well as resident. Antigua: The Excelsior Printery, 1939. 149 p., illus.

LITCHFIELD, LAWRENCE, JR. Bauxite. *Chemical Industries,* Vol. XLVIII, No. 2, February 1941. p. 154-9, illus. Also Part II, Vol. XLVIII, No. 3, March 1941. p. 290-5, illus.

————. The bauxite industry of northern South America. *Engineering and Mining Journal,* Vol. 128, No. 7, August 17, 1929. p. 242-8, illus., map.

————. Bauxite mining in Dutch Guiana. *Engineering and Mining Journal,* Vol. 128, No. 12, September 21, 1929. p. 460-4, illus.

MACGOWAN, H. P. Markets of the Dutch West Indies. United States Department of Commerce. Bureau of Foreign and Domestic Commerce. *Trade Information Bulletin,* No. 405. Washington: 1926. 26 p.

MORAN, LIEUTENANT COMMANDER CHARLES. The evolution of Caribbean strategy. *United States Naval Institute Proceedings,* Vol. 68, No. 469, March 1942. p. 365-73.

Netherlands. Ministry of Foreign Affairs. Economic Section. Holland and her colonies: economic guide book. Amsterdam: D. Y. Alta [, 1924]. 171 p.

————. Supplement [to Holland and her colonies], 1926. 14 p.

Netherlands West Indies. *Commercial and Financial Chronical,* Vol. 152, No. 3958, May 3, 1941. p. 2762-5.

NEWTON, ARTHUR PERCIVAL. The European nations in the West Indies, 1493-1688. The Pioneer Histories, edited by V. T. Harlow and J. A. Williamson. London: A. & C. Black, Ltd., 1933. 357 p.

PALGRAVE, WILLIAM GIFFORD. Dutch Guiana. London: Macmillan and Co., 1876. 260 p., map and plan.

PLATT, RAYE R. A note on political sovereignty and administration in the Caribbean. *Geographical Review,* New York, Vol. XV, October 1926. p. 623-37, 5 maps.

PLATT, RAYE R., WRIGHT, JOHN K. & OTHERS. The European possessions in the Caribbean area. A compilation of facts concerning their population, physical geography, resources, industries, trade, government, and strategic importance. Map of Hispanic America publication No. 4. New York: American Geographical Society, 1941. 106 p., map, bibl.

PRICE, A. GRENFELL. White settlers in the tropics. With additional notes by Robert G. Stone. American Geographical Society, Special Publication, No. 23. New York: American Geographical Society, 1939. 301 p., illus., bibl.

REDFIELD, A. H. The Petroleum trade of the Netherland West Indies. Supplement to *International Petroleum Trade,* Vol. 7, No. 11, November 25, 1938. 37 p., bibl.

> Prepared in the Petroleum Economics Division in cooperation with Foreign Minerals Division, U. S. Department of the Interior, Bureau of Mines, Economics and Statistics Branch.

RODWAY, JAMES. The West Indies and the Spanish Main. London: T. Fisher Unwin, 1896. 365 p., illus., map.

——————. Guiana, British, Dutch and French. London: T. Fisher Unwin, Ltd., 1921. 308 p., illus., map, bibl.

——————. In the Guiana forest. Studies of nature in relation to the struggle for life. London: T. Fisher Unwin, 1897. 326 p., illus.

——————. Guiana, the wild and the wonderful. *Timehri,* Vol. II, Third Series, No. 2, December 1912. p. 235-42, illus.

ROTH, WALTER E. An inquiry into the animism and folk-lore of the Guiana Indians. Extract from the thirtieth annual report of the Bureau of American Ethnology. Washington: Government Printing Office, 1915. p. 109-386, bibl.

SACK, BARON ALBERT VON. A narrative of a voyage to Surinam; of a residence there during 1805, 1806, and 1807; and of the author's return to Europe by way of North America. London: Printed for G. and W. Nicol, 1810. 282 p., 3 plates.

SLUITER, ENGEL. Dutch Guiana: a problem in boundaries. *The His-*

panic American Historical Review, Vol. XIII, No. 1, February 1933. p. 2-22, bibl.

STEDMAN, CAPT. J. G. Narrative of a five years' expedition against the revolted Negroes of Surinam, in Guiana, on the wild coast of South America; from the year 1772 to 1777: Elucidating the history of that country, and describing its productions, viz. quadrupedes, birds, fishes, reptiles, trees, shrubs, fruits, and roots; with an account of the Indians of Guiana, & Negroes of Guinea. Illustrated with 80 elegant engravings, from drawings made by the author. London: Printed for J. Johnson, 1796. 2 v., maps.

VANDERCOOK, JOHN W. Tom-Tom. New York: Harper & Brothers, Publishers, 1926. 258 p., illus.

WARDLAW, C. W. Agriculture in Suriname. *Tropical Agriculture,* the Official Journal of the Imperial College of Tropical Agriculture, Trinidad, B. W. I., Vol. VII, No. 2, February 1930. p. 31-7, illus.

WILLIAMS, JOSEPH J. Voodoos and obeahs. Phases of West India witchcraft. New York: The Dial Press, 1938. 257 p., bibl.

WOODSON, CARTER G. Negro slavery. *In* European civilization, its origin and development. Edward Eyre, Editor. Vol. VII; the relations of Europe with non-European peoples. New York: Oxford University Press, 1939. p. 555-93.

MAPS

Kaart van Surinam, scale 1:200,000. Compiled by L. A. Bakhuis and W. de Quant. The Hague: Published by commission of the Department of Colonies, 1930. 16 sheets.

Largest scale map of Surinam available.

Topographische Kaart van Curaçao, scale 1:20,000. The Hague, Topographic Institute [, 1922-3?]. 18 sheets.

Most detailed map of Curaçao available.

Topographische Kaart van Aruba, scale 1:20,000. The Hague, Topographic Institute [, 1918?]. 8 sheets.

Most detailed map of Aruba available.

Topographische Kaart van Bonaire, scale 1:20,000. The Hague, Topographic Institute [, 1932?]. 10 sheets.

Most detailed map of Bonaire available.

West Indië, scale 1:250,000; *also* St. Martin, Saba and St. Eustatius, scale 1:75,000; *and* Philipsburg, St. Martin and Oranjestad, St. Eustatius, scale 1:15,000. The Hague: Ministry of Marine, Hydrographic Department, 1926.

Most detailed map of the Netherlands Windward Islands available.

NEWSPAPERS AND PERIODICALS

DAILY

Curaçao: *Beurs en Nieuwsberichten,* in Dutch; *Boletin Comercial,* in Dutch, Spanish, and English; *Dagblad Amigoe di Curaçao,* in Dutch; *La Prensa,* in Dutch, Spanish, and English.

Aruba: *Aruba Post,* in Dutch and English: *El Despertador,* in Spanish and English.

TWICE WEEKLY

Surinam: *Suriname, De Surinamer, De Surinaamsche Bode, De West, Nieuwe Surinaamsche Courant, Onze West.*

WEEKLY

Curaçao: *La Cruz,* in Papiamento: *De Curaçaosche Courant,* in Dutch, and occasional articles in English; *La Union,* in Papiamento; *Weekblad Curaçao,* in Dutch, and occasional articles in English and other languages.

Surinam: *Official Gazette, The Weekly Echo.*

New York: *Knickerbocker Weekly,* in English and Dutch. Published at 30 Rockefeller Plaza.

FORTNIGHTLY

Windward Islands: *De Bovenwindsche Stemmen—Voices of the Windward Islands,* stencilled paper in English.

New York: *Netherlands News,* in English. Published by The Netherlands Information Bureau.

MONTHLY

Curaçao: *Oost en West, Publicatie-Blad* (Government bulletin).

The Hague: *West-Indische Gids.*

ANNUALLY

Curaçao: Curaçao report. II. Statistical annual of Curaçao for the year[s] 1927-37. (Curaçaosch verslag.) 's Gravenhage: Gedrukt ter Algemeene Landsdrukkerij, 1928-38.

Surinam: Surinam report. II. Statistical annual of Surinam for the year[s] 1931-7. (Surinaamsch verslag.) 's Gravenhage: Gedrukt ter Algemeene Landsdrukkerij, 1932-8.

Index

217